Bibliography of the Writings of Edwin Muir

BIBLIOGRAPHY
OF THE WRITINGS OF
EDWIN MUIR

BY
ELGIN W. MELLOWN

UNIVERSITY OF ALABAMA PRESS

University, Alabama

KAYE & WARD LTD, LONDON

CONTENTS

PREFACE

THIS WORK in its first form (part of the bibliography for my University of London dissertation, *The Literary Achievement of Edwin Muir, A Study of His Poetry and Prose* [1962]) was patterned after Donald Gallup's *T. S. Eliot: A Bibliography* (New York, 1953); in revising it I have turned ever more frequently to the Rupert Hart-Davis "Soho Bibliographies" of twentieth-century writers; and I have finally recast it (but with of course the inevitable variations) in the form used by Miss B. J. Kirkpatrick in her *Bibliography of Virginia Woolf* (London, 1957). The primary difference between the two works is my placing of Mr. and Mrs. Muir's translations in a category by themselves: they are found in Section D, that part generally reserved in the "Soho Bibliographies" for translations of the author's work.

Since I have compiled this bibliography in order to assist students concerned with Edwin Muir and with twentieth-century literature, a review of its scope may be an additional help to many. Section A contains descriptions of all the books and pamphlets which Muir wrote, although obviously not of all impressions or reprints of each title. Since only in *We Moderns* and *Latitudes* are there textual differences in the American and English editions, I have consistently described the English edition first, even though for several books the American edition preceded the English. Under Section B, Muir's contributions to books, there are probably several additional titles which should be included, but the section may be considered fairly complete.

Muir wrote regularly for the *Athenæum*, the *Nation*, the *Spectator*, the *Listener*, the *Scotsman*, the *Observer*, and other journals: the account of such writings includes all signed work and many unsigned pieces identified from editors' MSS books. But Muir was a journalist for almost forty years, and the quantity and anonymous character of many of his periodical contributions preclude their identification. For example, he was the assistant editor of and a principal contributor to the London *New Age* in

7

the early nineteen-twenties, but I have been able to include here only
his signed articles and poems because, according to Dr. Wally Martin,
who has made extensive research into the history of the *New Age*, there
are no marked copies of the newspaper. Muir also wrote dramatic reviews for the Edinburgh *Scotsman* in 1920-1921; but Sir George Waters,
former editor of the newspaper, has informed me through Mr. Charles
Graves that there is no way to identify those reviews written by Muir.
This section of periodical contributions is probably least adequate in its
listings of contributions to Scottish and American newspapers during
the nineteen-twenties and thirties, and information about these or any
other additional works will be gratefully received. Ideally, perhaps, the
title of every work reviewed by Muir would be included. Actually, however, the number of books which he reviewed made lengthy study of all
of them impossible for him (in some of his fortnightly *Listener* reviews
of "New Novels" he considered a dozen or so books within the space of
half a page); and it would be foolish to suggest that every one of his
judgments is worth the reader's attention. My selection of titles is based
upon either the literary value or contemporary repute of the book reviewed; the value or uniqueness of Muir's comments upon it; or (with
an eye to future biographers) Muir's relationship to its author or subject.
In some cases however I have given two or more titles merely to indicate
the range of the particular review. Cross-references are provided for the
titles of books in series and for those which Muir reviewed more than
once.

Section D may be taken as complete in its listing of titles, though not
of editions of these titles. Since Mr. and Mrs. Muir worked together so
closely in making these translations, I have also included works published
under Mrs. Muir's name or pseudonym. The thoughtful reader will com-
pare the dates of the translations by the Muirs with the dates of Edwin
Muir's original compositions and will decide for himself the proportion
of Mr. and Mrs. Muir's individual labors in the translating.

The Index which I have supplied has been designed not merely to
assist in the location of works, but also to supplement the Index of First
Lines in the *Collected Poems* and to provide a means of showing in one
place the different publications of a poem or essay. In every case I have
used the author's last title of the work for the main entry, giving cross
references under earlier titles or first lines. Thus every main entry provides the means of determining the various stages (if any) in the development of a poem or essay.

I must stress that this bibliography covers only the printed word and point out that it gives no account of the MSS materials which Mrs. Muir has deposited in the National Library of Scotland; of those still in her possession, including the lectures which Muir gave at Bristol and elsewhere; of his broadcast talks for the BBC, recordings or transcripts of which are to be found in the BBC archives; or of his recordings of his poems, which he made in the United States. Likewise I have not given any account of criticism concerning Muir and his work. The student who requires such information will find that Muir's books were reviewed by the leading literary periodicals in England and frequently in America as well. Lists of selected critical studies are provided by Mr. J. C. Hall in his admirable study *Edwin Muir*, No. 71 in the British Council "Writers and Their Work" series (1956), and by Professor Peter Butter in his *Edwin Muir*, in the Oliver and Boyd "Writers and Critics" series (1962).

This bibliography was compiled between the spring of 1959 and the winter of 1961-1962, principally in the Reading Room of the British Museum and the University of London Library. It was revised in the spring of 1964 at the University of Alabama. What completeness it has is due to the help of many persons, including:

Mrs. Willa Muir, who has discussed her husband's work with me, and who has given me much assistance in locating his early writings;

Professor Geoffrey Bullough, King's College (London), who directed the writing of the dissertation to which this work was originally attached; and

Mr. J. C. Hall and Professor Peter Butter, who have both written perceptively about Muir and who have discussed his work with me.

Dr. Wally Martin and Dr. Robert Hollander, students at London and Columbia, respectively, at the time I compiled this bibliography, have generously shared the results of their own research with me; and Mr. C. H. Peake, University College London, has read and commented upon the first version of the bibliography. To all of them my sincere thanks are freely given.

I am also grateful to the following persons for their replies to my often-times bothersome enquiries: Sir Stanley Unwin (Allen and Unwin, Ltd.); Mr. C. S. Nott (Janus Press); Mr. Charles Graves (*Scotsman*); Mrs. Freda Kirchwey (formerly of the *Nation*, New York); Mrs. Margaret Cole (one-time editor of the *Guild Socialist* and *New Standards*); Mr. I. M. Owen (Oxford University Press, Toronto); Miss Carla Packer

(Harcourt, Brace and World, Inc.); Miss R. DonCarlos (Clarke, Irwin and Co., Ltd.); Mr. Frank Flemington (Ryerson Press); and Miss Judy Rodnick (William Sloane Associates). For obtaining permission and making arrangements for me to inspect the marked copies of the *Spectator* and the *Athenæum*, I am grateful to Mr. C. A. Seaton, librarian of the *Spectator*, and to Mr. Jeremy Potter, manager of the *New Statesman*.

I gladly acknowledge my gratitude for the assistance given me by the staff members of the British Museum, the University of London Library, and King's College (London) Library. I have been helped with several special problems by Miss S. K. Forde (Harvard College Library), Mr. Frederick R. Goff (Library of Congress), Professor G. Thomas Tanselle (University of Wisconsin), and Mrs. S. E. G. Priestley, Crowborough, Sussex. The Interlibrary Loan Department of the University of Alabama Library has provided me with many of the American periodicals and editions here described, and to it and the libraries participating in the interlibrary loan service I express my thanks for their help and co-operation.

During 1960-1961 I received grants from the Southern Fellowships Fund and the University of Alabama: I am grateful for their assistance.

To my wife I once more give my thanks for the sacrifices she has made in order that this work could be finished.

ELGIN W. MELLOWN

May 1, 1964

A. BOOKS AND PAMPHLETS

In the following collations the asterisk (*) represents any ornament, including rules and publishers' devices.

A. BOOKS AND PAMPHLETS

A1   WE MODERNS   1918

a. First English Edition

WE MODERNS: | ENIGMAS AND GUESSES | BY | EDWARD
MOORE | * | LONDON: GEORGE ALLEN & UNWIN LTD. |
RUSKIN HOUSE 40 MUSEUM STREET, W. C. 1

248 pp.   6½ x 4 in.

P. [1] half-title; p. [2] blank; p. [3] title; p. [4] First published in 1918 |
(All Rights Reserved); p. [5] Dedication: To | A. R. Orage | Editor of
the *New Age*; p. [6] blank; p. 7, Preface (2 paragraphs signed Edward
Moore); p. [8] blank; p. 9, contents; p. [10] blank; p. [11] section
title; p. [12] blank; pp. 13-247, text (includes for each section a title
page on an unnumbered recto, with text of the section beginning on
next recto. Verso of each title is blank.); p. [248] Printed in Great Britain
by | Unwin Brothers, Limited | Woking and London

Blue, pebble-grained cloth boards; white paper label on spine lettered in
red: * | WE MODERNS | BY | EDWARD MOORE | GEORGE
ALLEN | & UNWIN LTD | * ; all edges trimmed; end-papers.

Published June, 1918.   4s. 6d.

1030 copies printed, of which 190 unbound copies were destroyed by
enemy action in 1940. In 1960 Bertram Rota, the specialist book-seller,
bought the remaining copies. Later bindings of this work include blue,
smooth cloth boards with white paper label on spine lettered (as above)
in blue.

CONTENTS: Six sections with numbered and titled paragraphs. I. The
Old Age (Nos. 1-37); II. Original Sin (Nos. 38-63); III. What is Mod-

ern? (Nos. 64-97); IV. Art in Literature (Nos. 98-143); V. Creative Love (Nos. 144-186); VI. The Tragic View (Nos. 187-209). Appendix: 16 epigrams.

b. First American edition. 1920

THE FREE LANCE BOOKS. IV | EDITED WITH INTRODUC- TIONS BY H. L. MENCKEN | * | WE MODERNS: | ENIGMAS AND GUESSES | BY EDWIN MUIR | * | * | NEW YORK AL- FRED · A · KNOPF MCMXX | * [Design includes three vertical rules]

244 pp.   7¼ x 5 in.

P. [1] half-title; p. [2] list of The Free-Lance Books; p. [3] title; p. [4] Copyright, 1920, by | Alfred A. Knopf, Inc. | Printed in the United States of America; p. [5] contents; p. [6] blank; pp. 7-21, Introduction signed H. L. Mencken; p. [22] blank; p. [23] section title; p. [24] blank; pp. 25-244, text (includes for each section a title page on an unnumbered recto, with text of the section beginning on next recto. Verso of each title is blank.)

Light-green paper boards, front cover printed in black: IV. WE MOD- ERNS | BY EDWIN MUIR | * | THE FREE-LANCE BOOKS. ED- ITED BY H. L. MENCKEN (with ornamented border and rules); black cloth spine with white paper label printed in black: * | WE | MODERNS | * | EDWIN MUIR | 1920 | * ; all edges trimmed; end- papers.

Published (before May) 1920. $1.75.

CONTENTS: As for A1*a*, with these exceptions: There are at least fourteen minor textual changes in A1*b*, most of them being omissions of Muir's parochial references to G. K. Chesterton. The Appendix (16 epigrams) is not included in A1*b*.

A2   LATITUDES   1924

a. First English Edition

LATITUDES | * | BY | EDWIN MUIR | LONDON: ANDREW MELROSE LTD. | 3 YORK STREET, COVENT GARDEN, W. C. 2.

[x], 322 pp.   7¾ x 5 in.

One blank leaf; p. [i] half-title; p. [ii] blank; p. [iii] title; p. [iv] Printed in U. S. A.; p. [v] Dedication: To | Adrian Collins; p. [vi] Author's Preface to the English Edition (4 paragraphs); p. [vii] acknowledgments; p. [viii] blank; p. [ix] contents; p. [x] blank; pp. 1-322, text; one blank leaf.

Rough blue cloth boards; white paper label on spine lettered in black with yellow rules: LATITUDES | EDWIN | MUIR | MELROSE; front cover stamped in blind with publisher's device and rules; top edges trimmed and colored, other edges untrimmed; purple cord bookmark bound in; end-papers.

Published October, 1924.   9s.

CONTENTS: Robert Burns. A Note on the Scottish Ballads. George Douglas. A Note on Mr. Conrad. A Note on Dostoyevsky. A Note on Ibsen. A Note on Friedrich Nietzsche. A Plea for Psychology in Literary Criticism. North and South. The Truth about Art. De l'Amour. The Affirmation of Suffering. Against Profundity. The Reign of Superstition. The Story of the Hungry Sheep. In Defense of New Truths. Against the Wise. Against Optimism and Pessimism. Against Being Convinced. Beyond the Absolute. On the Universe. Impressions of Prague. Reflections and Conjectures.

b. First American Edition.   1924

LATITUDES | * | BY | EDWIN MUIR | * | NEW YORK B. W. HUEBSCH, INC. MCMXXIV

[x], 322 pp.   7¼ x 5 in.

(Identical with A2a, with these exceptions: p. [iii] title; p. [iv] Copyright, 1924, by | B. W. Huebsch, Inc. | * | Printed in U. S. A.; p. [vi] blank.)

Light-grey cloth boards; white paper label on spine lettered in black with olive colored rules: LATITUDES | EDWIN | MUIR | HUEBSCH; front cover stamped in blind with publisher's device; all edges trimmed and top colored; end-papers.

Published 1924. $2.00

CONTENTS: As for A2a.

A3   FIRST POEMS   1925

a. First English Edition

FIRST POEMS | EDWIN MUIR | * | PUBLISHED BY | LEONARD
& VIRGINIA WOOLF AT THE HOGARTH PRESS | 52 TAVI-
STOCK SQUARE, LONDON, W. C. 1 | 1925

75 pp.   7½ x 5 in.

P. [1] blank; p. [2] acknowledgments; p. [3] title; p. [4] Dedication: To
P. W. | Printed in Great Britain by | Neill & Co., Ltd., Edinburgh.; pp.
5-6, contents; p. [7] section title: Poems; p. [8] blank; pp. 9-74, [75]
text (includes section title: Ballads); p. [76] blank.

Marbled-paper boards with white paper label on front cover printed in
black: FIRST POEMS | EDWIN MUIR, in double ruled rectangle;
top edges trimmed; outer leaves of signatures [1] and 5 pasted down to
form end-papers.

Published April, 1925.   4s. 6d.

The "P. W." of the dedication is Mrs. Muir: the initials stand for the
poet's private name for her, *Peedie Willa.*

CONTENTS: I. *Poems:* Childhood. The Lost Land. Remembrance.
Horses. Houses. Maya. The Enchanted Prince. October at Hellbrünn.
Reverie. On the Mediterranean. An Ancient Song. Betrayal. Anatomy.
Logos. When the Trees Grow Bare. Autumn near Prague. Salzburg—
November. Grass. II. *Ballads:* Ballad of Hector in Hades. Ballad of Re-
birth. Ballad of Eternal Life. Ballad of the Nightingale. Ballad of the
Monk. Ballad of the Flood.

b. First American Edition.   1925

FIRST POEMS | EDWIN MUIR | * | NEW YORK | B. W.
HUEBSCH, INC. | MCMXXV

75 pp.   7½ x 5 in.

(Identical with A3*a*, with these exceptions: One blank leaf; p. [1] half-
title; p. [3] title.)

Black cloth boards with blind-stamped publisher's device on front cover; green paper label on spine lettered in black from head to tail: MUIR: FIRST POEMS; top edges trimmed; end-papers.

Published 1925. $1.50

CONTENTS: As for A3*a*.

A4   CHORUS OF THE NEWLY DEAD   1926

First Edition

CHORUS OF THE NEWLY | DEAD | EDWIN MUIR | * | PRINT-ED & PUBLISHED BY LEONARD & VIRGINIA | WOOLF AT THE HOGARTH PRESS, LONDON. 1926

16 pp. 8 x 5¼ in.

P. [1] title; p. [2] Dedication: To John Holms; pp. 3-16, text.

Marbled-paper covers with yellow label on front cover printed in black: CHORUS OF THE NEWLY DEAD | EDWIN MUIR, in double-ruled rectangle; no end-papers.

Published July, 1926. 3s.

This publication was one of those which Mr. and Mrs. Woolf printed by hand, and is therefore similar in appearance to their edition of T. S. Eliot's *The Waste Land*.

CONTENTS: Chorus. The Idiot. Chorus. The Beggar. Chorus. The Coward. Chorus. The Harlot. Chorus. The Poet. Chorus. The Hero. Chorus. The Mystic. Chorus.

A5   TRANSITION   1926

a. First English Edition

* | TRANSITION | ESSAYS | ON CONTEMPORARY LITERA-TURE | BY | EDWIN MUIR | 1926 | PUBLISHED BY LEONARD AND VIRGINIA WOOLF | AT THE HOGARTH PRESS, 52 TAVI-STOCK SQUARE, LONDON | *

xii, 218 pp. 7½ x 5 in.

P. [i] half-title; p. [ii] Also by Edwin Muir (two titles); p. [iii] title; p. [iv] Printed in U. S. A.; p. [v] Dedication: To | Francis George Scott | * ; p. [vi] blank; pp. vii-ix, Preface (four paragraphs signed E. M. | Montrose, Scotland); p. [x] blank; p. [xi] contents; p. [xii] blank; p. [1] Introductory: The Zeit Geist | * ; p. [2] blank; pp. 3-218, text (includes chapter title on an unnumbered recto for each chapter, with the text beginning on next recto. Verso of each title page is blank.)

Maroon cloth boards with white paper label on spine lettered in black: TRANSITION | EDWIN MUIR, in single rule rectangle; top edges trimmed; end-papers.

Published October, 1926. 7s. 6d.

CONTENTS: Introductory: The Zeit Geist. James Joyce. D. H. Lawrence. Virginia Woolf. Stephen Hudson. Aldous Huxley. Lytton Strachey. T. S. Eliot. Edith Sitwell. Robert Graves. Contemporary Poetry. Contemporary Fiction.

b. First American Edition. 1926

* | TRANSITION | ESSAYS | ON CONTEMPORARY LITERATURE | BY | EDWIN MUIR | * | NEW YORK THE VIKING PRESS MCMXXVI | *

xii, 218 pp. 7½ x 5 in.

(Identical with A5a, with these exceptions: p. [iii] title; p. [iv] * | Copyright, 1926, by the Viking Press, Inc. | Manufactured in the United States of America | By the Vail-Ballou Press, Inc., Binghamton, N. Y. | *)

Light-green cloth boards with white paper label on spine lettered in orange and green: * | TRANSITION | ESSAYS ON | CONTEMPORARY | LITERATURE | EDWIN MUIR | * | MCMXXVI | THE VIKING PRESS | * ; all edges trimmed and top colored; end-papers.

Published 1926. $2.00

CONTENTS: As for A5a.

A6   THE MARIONETTE   1927

a. First English Edition

THE MARIONETTE | BY | EDWIN MUIR | [Quotation, 4 lines] | PUBLISHED BY LEONARD & VIRGINIA WOOLF AT THE | HOGARTH PRESS, 52 TAVISTOCK SQUARE, LONDON, W. C. 1 | 1927

156 pp.   7¼ x 5 in.

P. [1] half-title; p. [2] blank; p. [3] title; p. [4] Printed in Great Britain by | Hazell, Watson & Viney, Ld., London and Aylesbury.; pp. 5-155, text; p. [156] blank; pp. [157-160] publisher's advertisements, integral.

Light tan cloth boards; spine lettered in gold: THE | MARIONETTE | EDWIN MUIR | HOGARTH PRESS; all edges trimmed and top colored; end-papers. Pale-green dust-jacket printed in red; wood-cut design on spine and front cover.

Published May, 1927.   6s.

CONTENTS: 15 chapters, no titles.

b. First American Edition.   1927

THE MARIONETTE, BY | EDWIN MUIR. PUBLISHED | BY THE VIKING PRESS | NEW YORK. MCMXXVII | * [blue ink] (all within a single-ruled rectangular frame)

[viii], 181 pp.   6¾ x 4 in.

P. [i] half-title; p. [ii] By Edwin Muir (three titles); p. [iii] title; p. [iv] Copyright, 1927, by the Viking Press, Inc. | Printed in the United States of America; p. [v] quotation, four lines; p. [vi] blank; p. [vii] half-title; p. [viii] blank; pp. 1-181, text; pp. [182-184] blank.

Blue, flexible, plastic-treated cloth covers; on front cover at lower right gold stamped signature: EDWIN MUIR, with line under Muir; spine lettered in light green: MUIR | * | THE | MARI- | -O- | NETTE | VIKING; all edges trimmed and top colored; blue silk bookmark bound in; end-papers.

Published 1929. $1.25

CONTENTS: As for A6a.

A7   THE STRUCTURE OF THE NOVEL   1928

a. First English Edition

THE STRUCTURE | OF THE NOVEL | EDWIN MUIR | * | PUB-
LISHED BY LEONARD & VIRGINIA WOOLF AT THE | HO-
GARTH PRESS, 52 TAVISTOCK SQUARE, LONDON, W. C. 1 |
1928

152 pp.   7½ x 5 in.

P. [1] Hogarth Lectures on Literature | * | The Structure of the | Novel;
p. [2] publisher's advertisement (list of seven titles in the Hogarth Lectures on Literature Series; four additional titles listed as "In Prepara-
tion"); p. [3] title; p. [4] Printed in Great Britain by | Neill & Co., Ltd.,
Edinburgh.; p. 5, contents; p. [6] blank; pp. 7-151, text; p. [152] blank.

Sewn in brown linen-paper covers lettered on front cover in red:
HOGARTH LECTURES | NO. 6 | THE STRUCTURE OF | THE
NOVEL | EDWIN MUIR | THE HOGARTH PRESS; all edges
trimmed; no end-papers.

Published November, 1928. 3s. 6d.

The Hogarth Lecture Series was edited by George Rylands and Leonard
Woolf.

CONTENTS: Lectures I, Novels of Action and Character; II, The Dramatic Novel; III, Time and Space; IV, The Chronicle; V, The Period
Novel and Later Developments; VI, Conclusion.

b. First American Edition.   1929

THE STRUCTURE | OF THE NOVEL | * | EDWIN MUIR | * | * |
HARCOURT, BRACE AND COMPANY | NEW YORK [The whole
enclosed in panels.]

152 pp.   7½ x 5 in.

(Identical with A7a, with these exceptions: p. [3] title; p. [4] Copyright, 1929, By | Harcourt, Brace and Company, Inc. | Printed in the United States of America | By Quinn & Boden Company, Inc., Rahway, N. J.)

Blue cloth boards; blind-stamped lettering on front cover: HOGARTH | LECTURES | ON | LITERATURE; spine lettered in orange: THE | STRUC- | TURE | OF | THE | NOVEL | EDWIN | MUIR; top edge trimmed; end-papers.

Published 1929. $1.25

CONTENTS: As for A7a.

A8   JOHN KNOX   1929

a. First English Edition

JOHN KNOX: | PORTRAIT OF A CALVINIST | BY | EDWIN MUIR | * | JONATHAN CAPE | THIRTY BEDFORD SQUARE | LONDON.

316 pp.   8 x 5½ in.

P. [i] half-title; p. [ii] blank; frontispiece facing p. [iii]; p. [iii] title; p. [iv] First published 1929 | Printed in Great Britain by J. and J. Gray | Edinburgh; p. [v] Dedication: To | Hugh M'Diarmid | In Admiration; p. [vi] quotation, 2 lines; p. vii, contents; p. viii, list of illustrations; pp. ix-x, Preface (3 paragraphs); pp. 11-312, text (illustrations facing pp. 65, 177, and 241); pp. 313-316, Index; two blank leaves.

Maroon cloth boards; spine lettered in gold: JOHN KNOX | * | E. MUIR | JONATHAN CAPE; all edges trimmed; end-papers.

Published June, 1929.   12s. 6d.

CONTENTS: Preface. Chapters I. The Riddle; II. St. Andrews and the Galleys; III. Knox Hardens; IV. The Prophet; V. The Frankfort Interlude; VI. The Scottish Visit; VII. Geneva; VIII. Hesitation at Dieppe; IX. Doubts, Threats and Predestination; X. Exasperation at Dieppe; XI. Mary of Guise; XII. Death of Mary of Guise; XIII. The Book of Discipline; XIV. Mary Stuart; XV. Downfall of Mary Stuart; XVI. The End; Appendix A. Knox and Scotland; Appendix B. Biographical. Index.

b. First American Edition. *1929*

JOHN KNOX: | PORTRAIT OF A CALVINIST | BY | EDWIN MUIR | * | THE VIKING PRESS | NEW YORK—1929

316 pp.   8 x 5½ in.

(Identical with A8*a*, with this exception: p. [iii] title.)

Black cloth boards; on front cover a blind-stamped panel in which is mounted a reduced reproduction (1.5 x 1.25 in.) on paper in rose and white of the frontispiece portrait; white paper label on spine lettered in black and rose: JOHN KNOX | PORTRAIT OF A | CALVINIST | BY | EDWIN MUIR; all edges trimmed and top colored; end-papers.

Published 1929. $3.50

CONTENTS: As for A8*a*.

A9   THE THREE BROTHERS   1931

a. First English Edition

THE | THREE | BROTHERS | BY | EDWIN MUIR | * | LONDON | WILLIAM HEINEMANN LTD

[viii], 344 pp.   7½ x 5 in.

P. [i] half-title; p. [ii] publisher's advertisement; p. [iii] title; p. [iv] First published 1931 | * | Printed in Great Britain | At the Windmill Press | Kingswood : : Surrey; p. [v] Dedication: To Willa; p. [vi] blank; p. [vii] contents; p. [viii] blank; p. [1] Book I | David; p. [2] blank; pp. 3-344, text (includes for Books II and III a title page on an unnumbered recto, with text beginning on next recto. Verso of each title is blank.)

Green grained-cloth boards; blind-stamped rules on front cover and blind-stamped publisher's device on back cover; spine lettered in gold: * | THE | THREE | BROTHERS | * | EDWIN MUIR | HEINEMANN | * ; all edges trimmed; end-papers.

Published February, 1931.   7s. 6d.

On p. 312 lines 9 and 11 are identical; line 9 is incorrect.

CONTENTS: Book I. David; Book II. David and Archie; Book III. David, Archie and Sandy.

b. First American Edition.   *1931*

THE | THREE | BROTHERS | BY | EDWIN MUIR | * | * | NEW YORK | DOUBLEDAY, DORAN & COMPANY INC. | 1931

[viii], 344 pp.   7½ x 5 in.

(Identical with A9a, with these exceptions: p. [ii] blank; p. [iii] title; p. [iv] All rights reserved | Printed in Great Britain.)

Black cloth boards; on front cover a blind-stamped panel in which is mounted a printed pen-and-ink drawing (3.9 x 2.35 in.) in black and green on white paper showing three male figures, a castle, a house, and a tree, and including in an oval frame the legend: THE | THREE | BROTHERS | BY EDWIN | MUIR; a similar paper label (2.8 x 1.3 in.) on the spine with the three figures omitted and including at the bottom: DOUBLEDAY | DORAN; all edges trimmed and top colored; end-papers.

Published 1931. $2.50

On p. 312 line 9 is corrected to read: " 'He told me all about it,' said David."

CONTENTS: As for A9a.

A10   SIX POEMS   1932

First Edition

SIX | POEMS [blue ink] | EDWIN MUIR | THE STATIONARY JOURNEY | THE FIELD OF THE POTTER. THE TRANCE | TRISTRAM CRAZED. TRANSMUTATION | THE FALL | THE SAMSON PRESS [blue ink] | MCMXXXII

22 pp.   9 x 7 in.

Two blank leaves; p. [1] title; p. [2] author's acknowledgments; p. [3] poem title: THE STATIONARY JOURNEY; pp. 4-22, text (includes a title page for each poem; the initial letter of each poem is printed in blue ink); p. [23] This book was printed by J. M. Shelmerdine & | Flora Grierson at the Samson Press, Stuart's Hill Cottage, | Warlingham, Surrey, and was finished in March 1932. | Composition and press-work by J. M. Shelmerdine. There | were printed 110 copies, in Caslon Old Face, Nos. 1-90 | being for sale. This is Number __. ; two blank leaves.

Blue and white wood-block printed paper boards; white linen half-binding; white paper label on spine lettered from head to tail: MUIR: SIX POEMS; handmade paper with deckled edges; end-papers.

Published April, 1932.   7s. 6d.

Many copies of this limited edition were destroyed in a fire at the Samson Press. The copy here described is No. 97, the British Museum copy.

CONTENTS: As on the title page.

A11   POOR TOM   1932

First Edition

POOR TOM | BY | EDWIN MUIR | * | LONDON | J. M. DENT & SONS LTD.

254 pp.   7½ x 5 in.

One blank leaf; p. [1] half-title; p. [2] By the same author (nine titles); p. [3] title; p. [4] Printed in Great Britain | By The Camelot Press Southampton; p. [5] section title: Part One; p. [6] blank; pp. 7-254, text (includes section titles for Parts Two and Three); two blank leaves.

Blue cloth boards; spine lettered in gold: POOR | TOM | EDWIN MUIR | [at tail, blind-stamped in blind-stamped ruled rectangle] DENT; all edges trimmed; end-papers.

Published September, 1932.   7s. 6d.

CONTENTS: Part One: Chapters I-IX (no titles); Part Two: Chapters X-XXI; Part Three: Chapters XXII-XXVII.

A12   VARIATIONS ON A TIME THEME   1934

First Edition

VARIATIONS | ON A TIME THEME | EDWIN MUIR | LONDON: J. M. DENT & SONS LTD.

32 pp.   7½ x 5½ in.

Pp. [1-2] blank; p. [3] half-title; p. [4] publisher's advertisement; p. [5] title; p. [6] All rights reserved | Set in Eric Gill's Perpetua type | and printed in Great Britain | by The Temple Press Letchworth | for | J. M. Dent & Sons Ltd. | Aldine House Bedford St. London | Toronto · Vancouver | Melbourne · Wellington | First Published 1934; p. [7] Dedication: To the memory of | John Ferrar Holms | 1897-1934; p. [8] quotation, 4 lines; p. 9, author's acknowledgments, dated January 1934; p. [10] blank; pp. 11-31, text; p. [32] Temple Press colophon.

Grey art-paper boards (later bindings have off-white art-paper boards), lettered on spine from head to tail in blue: VARIATIONS ON A TIME THEME EDWIN MUIR DENT; all edges trimmed; end-papers. Grey dust-jacket printed in black and blue with advertisements on back cover.

Published April, 1934.   2s. 6d.

The *Variations* is the second volume in a series entitled New Poetry; the works are uniformly bound in paper boards of varying colors. *Cf.* A16.

CONTENTS: Ten poems numbered I–X without titles.

A13   SCOTTISH JOURNEY   1935

First Edition

SCOTTISH JOURNEY | BY | EDWIN MUIR | * | LONDON: | WILLIAM HEINEMANN LTD | IN ASSOCIATION WITH | VICTOR GOLLANCZ LTD

[vi], 250 pp.   8 x 5¼ in.

P. [i] half-title; p. [ii] publisher's advertisement; p. [iii] title; p. [iv] First Published 1935 | Printed in Great Britain | At the Windmill Press, Kingswood, Surrey; p. [v] contents; p. [vi] blank; pp. 1-250, text.

Bright blue cloth boards; spine lettered in gold: SCOTTISH | JOURNEY | EDWIN | MUIR | HEINEMANN | * | GOLLANCZ; all edges trimmed; end-papers. Brown kraft-paper dust-jacket printed in purple and green with advertisement on back cover.

Published October, 1935.   7s. 6d.

In 1933 Messrs. Heinemann and Gollancz commissioned three "travel" books which were subsequently published in similar bindings; the first two were *English Journey* by J. B. Priestley and *European Journey* by

Sir Philip Gibbs; *Scottish Journey* was the third in the series. It was published in North America by the Ryerson Press (Toronto). The managing editor of the Press, Mr. Frank Flemington, has written to me that "I think you are safe in assuming that the edition which . . . we published of Muir's *Scottish Journey* is the same as . . . the English edition. We represented Heinemann at that time and merely published their edition in Canada." I have not been able to locate any copy of the book which can be distinguished from the English edition.

CONTENTS: Scottish Journey [introduction]. Chapters I. Edinburgh; II. The South; III. To Glasgow; IV. Glasgow; V. The Highlands; VI. Conclusion.

A14   SOCIAL CREDIT AND THE LABOUR PARTY   1935

First Edition

SOCIAL CREDIT | & | THE LABOUR PARTY | AN APPEAL | BY | EDWIN MUIR | STANLEY NOTT LTD | 69 GRAFTON STREET FITZROY SQUARE | LONDON

28 pp.   8½ x 5½ in.

P. [1] half-title; p. [2] blank; p. [3] title; p. [4] 1935 | Printed in Great Britain | By Western Printing Services Ltd., Bristol; pp. 5-28, text; one blank leaf.

Stapled in brown paper covers lettered on front cover in red: PAM-PHLETS ON | THE NEW ECONOMICS | NO. 15 | (nine lines as on title) | PRICE: SIXPENCE, the whole enclosed by a double-ruled rectangle; inside front cover list of the seventeen pamphlets in the series; publisher's advertisements on back cover, inside and out; all edges trimmed; no end-papers.

Published December, 1935.   6d.

A15   SCOTT AND SCOTLAND   1936

a. First English Edition

SCOTT AND | SCOTLAND | THE PREDICAMENT OF THE | SCOTTISH WRITER | BY | EDWIN MUIR | * | GEORGE ROUT-

LEDGE | AND SONS, LTD. BROADWAY | HOUSE, CARTER LANE, LONDON, E.C. | 1936

182 pp.   7½ x 5 in.

P. [1] half-title; p. [2] list of eight titles in the Voice of Scotland series; p. [3] title; p. [4] First published 1936 | Printed in Great Britain by T. and A. Constable Ltd. | at the University Press, Edinburgh; p. [5] contents; p. [6] blank; p. [7] author's acknowledgments; p. [8] blank; pp. 9-181, [182] text; one blank leaf.

Light green cloth boards; on front cover a blind-stamped thistle; spine lettered in gold: SCOTT | AND | SCOTLAND | EDWIN | MUIR | ROUTLEDGE; all edges trimmed and top colored; end-papers.

Published September, 1936.   5s.

Scott and Scotland is the eighth and final volume in the Voice of Scotland series, the other works having been published by Routledge between September, 1935, and September, 1936. They are uniform in size and binding. A ninth title, *Red Scotland* by "Hugh MacDiarmid," was announced in the earlier titles of the series, as well as an unnamed tenth volume, but neither was issued. Later titles (including *Scott and Scotland*) drop *Red Scotland* from the list of works in the Voice of Scotland series, yet retain the statement "And a tenth volume" to end the list.

CONTENTS: Introductory; I. Scottish Literature; II. Scott and Scotland; III. Conclusions.

b. First American Edition.   *1938*

SCOTT AND | SCOTLAND | THE PREDICAMENT OF THE | SCOTTISH WRITER | EDWIN MUIR | * | ROBERT SPELLER | NEW YORK

182 pp.   7¼ x 5 in.

(Identical with A15a, with these exceptions: p. [3] title; p. [4] First published 1938 | by | Robert Speller Publishing Corp.)

Blue, plastic-treated cloth boards; front cover stamped in bright blue: SCOTT | AND | SCOTLAND | EDWIN MUIR; spine stamped in bright blue: SCOTT | & | SCOTLAND | MUIR | * | ROBERT | SPELLER; all edges trimmed; end-papers.

Published 1938. $2.00

Leaf A₂ (pp. [3-4]) is tipped in.

CONTENTS: As for A15a.

A16   JOURNEYS AND PLACES   1937

First Edition

JOURNEYS AND PLACES | EDWIN MUIR | LONDON: J. M. DENT & SONS LTD.

x, 54 pp.   7½ x 5½ in.

P. [i] half-title; p. [ii] publisher's advertisement; p. [iii] title; p. [iv] All rights reserved | Set in Eric Gill's Perpetua type | and printed in Great Britain | by The Temple Press Letchworth | for | J. M. Dent & Sons Ltd. | Aldine House Bedford St. London | Toronto · Vancouver | Melbourne · Wellington | First Published 1937; p. [v] Dedication: To | Flora Grierson and Joan Shelmerdine; p. [vi] blank; pp. vii-viii, Author's Note (five paragraphs); pp. ix-x, contents; p. [1] section title: Journeys; p. [2] blank; pp. 3-53, text (includes section title, p. [21]: Places); p. [54] Temple Press colophon.

Grey art-paper boards; spine lettered in red from head to tail: JOUR-NEYS AND PLACES EDWIN MUIR DENT; all edges trimmed; end-papers.

Published September, 1937.   2s. 6d.

Journeys and Places is the seventeenth volume in the Dent New Poetry series. *Cf.* A12.

CONTENTS: I. Journeys: The Stationary Journey. The Mountains. The Hill. The Road. The Mythical Journey. Tristram's Journey. Hölderlin's Journey. II. Places: The Fall. Troy I. Troy II. Judas. Merlin. The En-chanted Knight. Mary Stuart. Ibsen. The Town Betrayed. The Unfamiliar Place. The Place of Light and Darkness. The Solitary Place. The Private

Place. The Unattained Place. The Threefold Place. The Original Place. The Sufficient Place. The Dreamt-of Place.

A17   THE PRESENT AGE   1939

a. First English Edition

THE | PRESENT AGE | FROM 1914 | * | BY | EDWIN MUIR | * | THE CRESSET PRESS | LONDON

310 pp.   8 x 5 in.

Pp. [1-2] blank; p. [3] Introductions | to | English Literature | Edited by | Bonamy Dobrée | Volume V; p. [4] blank; p. [5] half-title; p. [6] blank; p. [7] title; p. [8] Printed in Guernsey, C. I. British Isles, | by The Star and Gazette Ltd.; p. [9] Note, signed E. M. (three paragraphs); p. [10] blank; p. [11] contents; p. [12] blank; pp. 13-20, Editor's Preface (for the series); pp. 21-22, Editor's Note to Volume V; pp. 23-302, text; pp. 303-309, Index of Names; p. [310] blank; one blank leaf.

Light olive cloth boards; spine lettered in blue: THE | PRESENT | AGE | * | EDWIN | MUIR | CRESSET | PRESS; all edges trimmed; end-papers.

Published April, 1939.   7s. 6d.

CONTENTS: Notes and Prefaces (as above); Chapters I. General Background; II. Poetry; III. Fiction; IV. General Prose; V. Criticism; VI. Drama; VII. Conclusion; Bibliography: Poetry, Fiction, Drama, General Prose, War Books. Index of Names.

b. First American Edition.   1940

THE | PRESENT AGE | FROM 1914 | * | BY | EDWIN MUIR | * | ROBERT M. MC BRIDE AND COMPANY | NEW YORK

310 pp.   8 x 5 in.

(Identical with A17*a*, with these exceptions: p. [7] title; p. [8] Copyright, 1940, by | Robert M. McBride and Company | All rights to reprint any material from | this book are reserved by the publisher | First

Edition, 1940 | Printed in Guernsey, Channel Islands, British | Isles by the Star and Gazette Limited.)

Brown cloth boards; spine lettered in gold: THE | PRESENT | AGE | * | MUIR | MC BRIDE; all edges trimmed; end-papers.

Published 1940. $2.75

Leaf A4 (pp. [7-8]) is tipped in.

CONTENTS: As for A17a.

A18   THE STORY AND THE FABLE   1940

First Edition

THE | STORY & THE FABLE | AN AUTOBIOGRAPHY | BY | EDWIN MUIR | * | GEORGE G. HARRAP & CO. LTD. | LONDON TORONTO BOMBAY SYDNEY

[iv], 264 pp.   8¾ x 5½ in.

P. [i] half-title; p. [ii] blank; frontispiece (photograph of Edwin Muir) facing p. [iii]; p. [iii] title; p. [iv] First published 1940 | by George G. Harrap & Co. Ltd. | 182 High Holborn, London, W. C. 1 | Copyright. All rights reserved | * | Made in Great Britain. Printed by J. and J. Gray, Edinburgh; p. [1] Dedication: To | Stanley Cursiter | and | Eric Linklater | Fellow-Orkneymen; p. [2] blank; p. 3, Preface (two paragraphs, signed E. M., April, 1940); p. [4] blank; p. 5, contents; p. [6] blank; p. [7] half-title; p. [8] blank; pp. 9-263, [264] text.

Blue-green cloth boards, front cover blind-stamped with rules and ornaments; spine lettered in white: THE | STORY | AND THE | FABLE | AN | AUTOBIOGRAPHY | EDWIN | MUIR | HARRAP; all edges trimmed; end-papers.

Published May, 1940.   11s.

The CBI lists an edition of *The Story and the Fable* published by the Oxford University Press, Toronto; but the manager of the Canadian branch of the Press, Mr. I. M. Owen, has informed me that "we have no record of our having done an edition ourselves, and it seems most improbable that we would have. . . . We were Harrap's exclusive agent in

Canada in 1940, . . . and I am confident that we simply distributed the Harrap edition."

CONTENTS: Chapters I. Wyre; II. Garth; III. Glasgow; IV. Fairport; V. London; VI. Prague and Dresden; VII. Extracts from a Diary, 1937-39.

A19   THE NARROW PLACE   1943

First Edition

THE NARROW PLACE | BY | EDWIN MUIR | FABER AND FABER LIMITED | 24 RUSSELL SQUARE | LONDON

50 pp.   8¼ x 5½ in.

P. [1] half-title; p. [2] blank; p. [3] title; p. [4] First published in Mcmxliii | by Faber and Faber Limited | 24 Russell Square London W. C. 1 | Printed in Great Britain by | R. MacLehose and Company Limited | The University Press Glasgow | All rights reserved; p. 5, contents; p. 6, author's acknowledgments; pp. 7-50, text; one blank leaf.

Blue cloth boards; spine lettered in gold from head to tail: THE NARROW PLACE EDWIN MUIR FABER; no edges trimmed; end-papers.

Published February, 1943.   6s.

CONTENTS: I, The Narrow Place: To J. F. H. (1897-1934). The Wayside Station. The River. Then. The Refugees. Scotland 1941. The Letter. The Human Fold. The Narrow Place. The Recurrence. The Good Man in Hell. The Wheel. The Face. The Law. The City. The Grove. The Gate. The Little General. The Prize. The Shades. The Ring. II, Postscript: Isaiah. The Return. Robert the Bruce. The Trophy. The Annunciation. The Confirmation. The Commemoration. The Old Gods. The Bird. The Guess. The Swimmer's Death. The Question. The Day.

A20   THE SCOTS AND THEIR COUNTRY   1946

First Edition

[Cover title] THE SCOTS | AND THEIR | COUNTRY | BY | EDWIN MUIR | 1/- NET

32 pp.   8¼ x 6 in.

P. [1] front cover, title with colored illustration; p. [2] map of Scotland in black and white; pp. 3-31, text, with numerous illustrations in text and full-page; p. [32] outside back cover: advertisement listing ten titles in the series The British People; also at bottom: British Council Code Name—SCOTSCO Longmans' Code Number (1)00008 | Printed in England by The Sun Engraving Company, Limited, London and Watford.

Stapled in illustrated paper covers; all edges trimmed; no end-papers.

Published April, 1946.   1s.

The Scots and Their Country is the eighth pamphlet in a series of eleven published between 1945 and 1948 under the general title, *The British People, How They Live and Work.* Each work was commissioned by the British Council.

CONTENTS: Essay.

A21   THE VOYAGE   1946

First Edition

THE VOYAGE AND | OTHER POEMS | BY | EDWIN MUIR | FABER AND FABER | LONDON

54 pp.   9 x 6 in.

P. [1] half-title; p. [2] Also by Edwin Muir | * | The Narrow Place; p. [3] title; p. [4] Dedication: To | Lumir and Catriona | First published in Mcmxlvi | by Faber and Faber Limited | 24 Russell Square London, W. C. 1 | Printed in Great Britain by | R. MacLehose and Company Limited | The University Press Glasgow | All rights reserved; pp. 5-6, contents; pp. 7-53, text; p. [54] blank; one blank leaf.

Light-blue cloth boards; spine lettered in gold from head to tail: THE VOYAGE & OTHER POEMS BY EDWIN MUIR FABER; watermark on paper: HAND MADE J. GREEN & SON; top edges trimmed; end-papers. Grey dust-jacket printed in blue and black; publisher's advertisements on back cover.

Published April, 1946. 6s.

CONTENTS: The Return. The Escape. The Castle. Moses. Sappho. The Covenant. Thought and Image. Twice-Done, Once-Done. Dialogue. The Voyage. The Fathers. The Three Mirrors. The Rider Victory. The Window. The House. The Myth. On Seeing Two Lovers in the Street. Song. Suburban Dream. Reading in Wartime. The Lullaby. Dejection. Song of Patience. Song. Sorrow. Epitaph. Comfort in Self-Despite. The Transmutation. Time Held in Time's Despite. To Ann Scott-Moncrieff (1914-1943). A Birthday. All We. In Love for Long.

A22   THE POLITICS OF KING LEAR   1947

First Edition

THE POLITICS OF | KING LEAR | THE SEVENTH W. P. KER MEMORIAL LECTURE DELIVERED | IN THE UNIVERSITY OF GLASGOW | 23RD APRIL, 1946 | BY | EDWIN MUIR | DIRECTOR OF THE BRITISH INSTITUTE, PRAGUE | * | GLASGOW | JACKSON, SON & COMPANY | PUBLISHERS TO THE UNIVERSITY | 1947

24 pp. 8½ x 5½ in.

P. [1] Glasgow University Publications | LXXII | The Politics of King Lear; p. [2] blank; p. [3] title; p. [4] blank; pp. [5], 6-24, text; p. 24, Printed in Great Britain by | Robert MacLehose and Co. Ltd. | The University Press, Glasgow, | For Jackson, Son and Co. (Booksellers) Ltd. | Publishers to the University | Glasgow. Stapled in brown paper covers lettered on front cover in black: [as on title page]; on back cover list of six previous lectures; all edges trimmed.

Published September, 1947. 2s.

A23   ESSAYS ON LITERATURE AND SOCIETY   1949

First Edition

ESSAYS ON | LITERATURE AND | SOCIETY | BY | EDWIN MUIR | * | LONDON | THE HOGARTH PRESS | 1949

168 pp. 8 x 5 in.

P. [1] half-title; p. [2] By the same Author | * | The Structure of the
Novel; p. [3] title; p. [4] Published by | The Hogarth Press Ltd. | Lon-
don | * | Clarke, Irwin & Company Ltd. | Toronto | Produced in com-
plete con- | formity with the author- | ised economy standards | Printed
in Great Britain | All Rights Reserved; pp. 5-6, contents; pp. 7-165, text;
pp. 166-[168] Index; p. [168] Printed in Great Britain | By R. & R. Clark,
Ltd., Edinburgh.

Blue cloth boards; spine lettered in gold: ESSAYS | ON | LITERA- |
TURE | & | SOCIETY | * | EDWIN | MUIR | THE | HOGARTH |
PRESS; top and side edges trimmed; end-papers. Pale-blue dust-jacket
printed in blue; publisher's advertisements on back cover.

Published May, 1949.   8s. 6d.

Dufour Editions issued this work in the U. S. A., affixing its label on
the inside front cover of the Hogarth Press edition. The label (which
would more logically have been placed on the title page) is green paper,
1 x 3 inches with rounded ends, and is lettered in white: PUBLISHED
IN THE UNITED STATES BY | DUFOUR EDITIONS | 3327
CHESTNUT STREET PHILADELPHIA 4, PA. I am informed by
Miss R. DonCarlos, Executive Assistant to the Editor, Clarke, Irwin and
Co. Ltd., that this press has merely been an agent for the Hogarth Press
and "has never published an independent edition" of any of Muir's
works.

CONTENTS: Robert Henryson. "Royal Man:" Notes on the Tragedies
of George Chapman. The Politics of *King Lear* (The W. P. Ker Lecture
for 1946, given in the University of Glasgow). Laurence Sterne. Burns
and Popular Poetry. Walter Scott (The Walter Scott Lecture for 1944,
given at the University of Edinburgh). Friedrich Hölderlin. Hölderlin's
Patmos. Robert Browning. The Novels of Thomas Hardy. Franz Kafka.
Oswald Spengler. The Political View of Literature. The Decline of the
Novel. The Natural Man and the Political Man. Index.

A24   THE LABYRINTH   1949
First Edition

THE LABYRINTH | BY | EDWIN MUIR | FABER AND FABER |
24 RUSSELL SQUARE | LONDON

62 pp.   8½ x 5½ in.

Pp. [1-2] blank; p. [3] half-title; p. [4] By the same author | * | The Narrow Place | The Voyage; p. [5] title; p. [6] First published in mcmxlix | by Faber and Faber Limited | 24 Russell Square London W. C. 1 | Printed in Great Britain by | R. MacLehose and Company Limited | The University Press Glasgow | All rights reserved; p. 7, contents; p. [8] blank; pp. 9-61, text; p. [62] blank; one blank leaf.

Blue cloth boards; spine lettered in gold from head to tail: THE LABYRINTH BY EDWIN MUIR * FABER; all edges trimmed; endpapers. Grey dust-jacket printed in black and red; publisher's advertisements on back cover.

Published June, 1949.   8s. 6d.

CONTENTS: Too Much. The Labyrinth. The Way. The Return. The West. The Journey Back. The Bridge of Dread. The Helmet. The Child Dying. The Combat. The Intercepter. Head and Heart. The Interrogation. The Border. The Good Town. The Usurpers. The Bargain. Oedipus. Circle and Square. Love's Remorse. Love in Time's Despite. Soliloquy. The Absent. The Visitor. The Transfiguration. The Debtor. Song. The Toy Horse.

A25   COLLECTED POEMS, 1921-1951   1952

a. First English Edition

EDWIN MUIR | COLLECTED POEMS | 1921-1951 | FABER AND FABER | 24 RUSSELL SQUARE | LONDON

196 pp.   8 x 5¼ in.

P. [1] half-title; p. [2] Poetry by Edwin Muir | published by Faber & Faber | (three titles); p. [3] title; p. [4] First published in mcmlii | by Faber and Faber Limited | 24 Russell Square London W. C. 1 | Printed in Great Britain by | R. MacLehose and Company Limited | The University Press Glasgow | All rights reserved; pp. 5-8, contents; pp. 9-14, Introduction (nine paragraphs) signed J. C. Hall June 1951; p. 14, Author's Note (two paragraphs) signed E. M.; p. [15] book title: First Poems; p. [16] blank; pp. 17-192, text (includes book title on an unnumbered recto for each work included, with the text beginning on the next recto. Verso of each book title is blank.); pp. 193-96, Index of First Lines.

Blue-green cloth boards; spine lettered in gold: * | COLLECTED |
POEMS | * | EDWIN | MUIR | * | FABER; all edges trimmed; end-
papers.

Published June, 1952.   15s.

The suggestion of issuing a collected edition of his poems was made to
Muir by Mr. J. C. Hall, a member of the *Encounter* staff and a poet
himself; and it was Hall who at Muir's request edited the volume. His
assistance was acknowledged by Muir in the "Author's Note" to *Collected Poems, 1921-1958* (A29).

CONTENTS: From *First Poems* (A3): Childhood. Horses. Betrayal.
When the Trees Grow Bare. Autumn in Prague. Ballad of Hector in
Hades. From *Variations on a Time Theme* (A12): Numbers II, VI, IX,
X (without numbers). All poems from *Journeys and Places* (A16) ex-
cept The Mythical Journey. Troy II. Judas. The Solitary Place. The Private
Place. The Threefold Place. The Original Place. The Sufficient Place. The
Dreamt-of Place. All poems from *The Narrow Place* (A19) except The
Refugees. Scotland 1941. The Narrow Place. The Wheel. The Shades.
Isaiah. The Question. All poems from *The Voyage* (A21) except Sappho.
Dialogue. The House. On Seeing Two Lovers in the Street. Song of
Patience. Song. All poems from *The Labyrinth* (A24). New Poems,
1949-1951: Adam's Dream. The Succession. Orpheus' Dream. The An-
nunciation. The Killing. The Island. One Foot in Eden. Day and Night.
The Animals. Index of First Lines.

b. First American Edition.   1953

EDWIN MUIR | COLLECTED POEMS | 1921-1951 | GROVE PRESS
| NEW YORK CITY

196 pp.   8 x 5¼ in.

(Identical with A25a, with these exceptions: p. [3] title; p. [4] First
published in mcmliii | by Grove Press | 795 Broadway | New York 3 |
Printed in Great Britain by | R. MacLehose and Company Limited | The
University Press Glasgow | All rights reserved | Copyright 1953 | Edwin
Muir.)

Blue-green cloth boards; spine lettered in gold: * | COLLECTED |

POEMS | * | EDWIN | MUIR | * | GROVE | PRESS; all edges trimmed; end-papers.

Published 1953. $3.50

CONTENTS: As for A25*a*.

A26   PROMETHEUS   1954

First Edition

[Cover title] ARIEL POEM | * | PROMETHEUS | BY | EDWIN MUIR | ILLUSTRATED BY | JOHN PIPER | * | FABER AND FABER

Covers, two leaves. 8½ x 5½ in.

Cover title; blank verso. First leaf, recto: black and white design containing the words PROMETHEUS | EDWIN MUIR; on verso a multicolor design. Second leaf (recto and verso): text. Inside back cover, black and white design; at foot of page: First published in mcmliv by Faber & Faber Limited, 24 Russell Square, London, WC 1 | Printed in Great Britain by Jesse Broad & Co. Ltd., Manchester. All rights reserved; on back cover, publisher's advertisement listing Ariel Poems (new series).

One sheet sewn in paper covers, outside cover yellow printed in black, inside white printed in black; all edges trimmed. Issued in light-green envelope lettered in black.

Published October, 1954. 2s.

A27   AN AUTOBIOGRAPHY   1954

a. First English Edition

AN | AUTOBIOGRAPHY | * | EDWIN MUIR | 1954 | THE HO-GARTH PRESS | LONDON

288 pp. 8½ x 5½ in.

P. [1] half-title; p. [2] By the Same Author (thirteen titles); p. [3] title; p. [4] Published by | The Hogarth Press Ltd | London | * | Clarke, Irwin

and Co. Ltd | Toronto | Printed in Great Britain | All Rights Reserved;
p. [5] Dedication: To | Stanley Cursiter | and | Eric Linklater | Fellow-
Orkneymen; p. [6] blank; p. 7, Preface (two paragraphs); p. 8, list of
illustrations; p. 9, contents; p. [10] map of the Orkney Islands; pp. 11-
281, text (illustrations facing pp. 14, 112, 188, and 264); pp. 282-[288]
Index; p. [288] Printed in Great Britain | by T. and A. Constable Ltd.,
Hopetoun Street, | Printers to the University of Edinburgh.

Red cloth boards; spine lettered in gold: [in a dark blue panel framed
in gold] AN | AUTO- | BIOGRAPHY | BY | EDWIN | MUIR | [at
tail without panel] THE | HOGARTH | PRESS; all edges trimmed and
top colored; end-papers. Red-brown dust-jacket printed in black and
white; picture of Muir on back cover.

Published October, 1954.   18s.

Clarke, Irwin and Co. Ltd. was the Canadian agent for the Hogarth Press
and never issued an independent edition of *An Autobiography*. For
further information see A23.

CONTENTS: Preface. Chapters 1. Wyre; 2. Garth; 3. Glasgow; 4.
Fairport; 5. London; 6. Prague; 7. Interval; 8. Dresden and Hellerau; 9.
Italy and Austria; 10. England and France; 11. Scotland; 12. Prague
Again; 13. Rome. Index.

b. First American Edition.   1954

AN | AUTOBIOGRAPHY | * | EDWIN MUIR | NEW YORK |
WILLIAM SLOANE ASSOCIATES, INC.

288 pp.   8½ x 5½ in.

(Identical with A27a, with these exceptions: p. [3] title; p. [4] Printed
in Great Britain | Copyright 1954 by Edwin Muir | All Rights Reserved.)

Light-rose cloth boards; spine lettered in gold as on A27a, but without
the dark blue background in panel, and at tail, SLOANE; all edges
trimmed and top colored; end-papers.

Published 1954. $5.00

Miss Judy Rodnick of William Sloane Associates (Subsidiary Rights Department) has informed me that this book was "a direct import from

the English publisher," that "sheets were imported . . . , but the binding, etc., was done here in this country."

CONTENTS: As for A27a.

A28   ONE FOOT IN EDEN   1956

a. First English Edition

EDWIN MUIR | ONE FOOT IN EDEN | FABER AND FABER | 24 RUSSELL SQUARE | LONDON

84 pp.   8½ x 5½ in.

Pp. [1-4] blank; p. [5] half-title; p. [6] by the same author (four titles); p. [7] title; p. [8] First published in mcmlvi | by Faber and Faber Limited | 24 Russell Square London W. C. 1 | Printed in Great Britain by | R. MacLehose and Company Limited | The University Press Glasgow | All rights reserved; p. [9] Dedication: To | Willa; p. [10] blank; pp. 11-12, contents; p. [13] section title: I; p. [14] blank; pp. 15-84, text (includes blank p. [51]; section title: II, p. [53]; and blank p. [54]).

Burgundy cloth boards; spine lettered in gold from head to tail: EDWIN MUIR * ONE FOOT IN EDEN * FABER; all edges trimmed; end-papers. Yellow dust-jacket printed in red and black; publisher's advertisements on back cover.

Published March, 1956.   10s. 6d.

CONTENTS: I: Milton. The Animals. The Days. Adam's Dream. Outside Eden. Prometheus. The Grave of Prometheus. Orpheus' Dream. The Other Oedipus. The Charm. Telemachos Remembers. The Heroes. Abraham. The Succession. The Road. The Annunciation. The Christmas. The Son. The Killing. Lost and Found. Antichrist. The Lord. One Foot in Eden. The Incarnate One. Scotland's Winter. The Great House. The Emblem. II: To Franz Kafka. Effigies. The Difficult Land. Nothing There but Faith. Double Absence. Day and Night. The Other Story. Dream and Thing. Song for a Hypothetical Age. The Young Princes. The Cloud. The Horses. Song. The Island. Into Thirty Centuries Born. My Own. The Choice. If I Could Know. The Late Wasp. The Late Swallow. Song.

b. First American Edition.   1956

EDWIN MUIR | ONE FOOT IN EDEN | GROVE PRESS NEW YORK

84 pp.   8 x 5½ in.

(Identical with A28a, with these exceptions: pp. [1-4] not included; p. [7] title; p. [8] First published in the United States, 1956, by | Grove Press, 795 Broadway, New York 3, N. Y. | All rights reserved. | One Foot in Eden is published in two editions: | An Evergreen Book of Poetry (E-38) | A hard bound limited edition of 200 copies | Library of Congress Catalog Card No. 56-5730 | Grove Press Books and Evergreen Books | are published by Barney Rosset | 795 Broadway New York, N. Y. | Manufactured in the United States of America.)

Sewn gatherings in stiff white paper covers; design on front cover in grey, orange, and black includes in horizontal type: ONE | FOOT | IN | EDEN | $1.45; and in vertical type: AN EVERGREEN BOOK PUB-LISHED BY GROVE PRESS | EDWIN MUIR; spine lettered in black from head to tail; ONE FOOT IN EDEN EDWIN MUIR E-38 * GROVE PRESS; inside front and back covers list printed in green of Evergreen Books; all edges trimmed.

CONTENTS: As for A28a.

A29 COLLECTED POEMS, 1921-1958 1960

a. First Edition

EDWIN MUIR | * | COLLECTED POEMS | 1921-1958 | FABER AND FABER | 24 RUSSELL SQUARE | LONDON

310 pp.   8 x 5¼ in.

P. [1] half-title; p. [2] by the same author (seven titles); frontispiece (photograph of Edwin Muir) facing p. [3]; p. [3] title; p. [4] Collected Poems 1921-1958 | first published in mcmlx | by Faber and Faber Limited | 24 Russell Square London W. C. 1 | Printed in Great Britain by | Western Printing Services Limited | All rights reserved | © This collection Willa Muir | 1960; p. [5] Dedication: To Willa; p. [6] blank; p. 7, Author's Note (two paragraphs) signed E. M.; pp. 7-8, Note on the Final Section (three paragraphs) signed Willa Muir and J. C. Hall; pp. 9-16, contents; p. [17] book title: First Poems | * | 1925; p. [18]

blank; pp. 19-301, text (includes book title on an unnumbered recto for each work included, with the text beginning on the next recto. Verso of each book title is blank.); p. [302] blank; pp. 303-310, Index of First Lines; one blank leaf.

Blue cloth boards; spine lettered in gold: EDWIN | MUIR | * | COL-LECTED | POEMS | 1921-1958 | FABER; all edges trimmed; end-papers. Light-blue dust-jacket printed in red and dark blue, publisher's advertisement on back cover.

Published April, 1960. 25s.

CONTENTS: From *First Poems* (A3): Childhood. Horses. Betrayal. When the Trees Grow Bare on the High Hills. Autumn in Prague. October at Hellbrünn. Ballad of Hector in Hades. Ballad of the Soul. Ballad of the Flood. All poems from *Variations On A Time Theme* (A12). All poems from *Journeys and Places* (A16) except Judas. All poems from *The Narrow Place* (A19) except Isaiah. All poems from *The Voyage* (A21) except Dialogue. Song. All poems from *The Laby-rinth* (A24). All poems from *One Foot in Eden* (A28) except The Christmas. The Son. Lost and Found. The Lord. The Choice. *Poems not previously collected:* I (Completed Poems), Sonnet ("You will not leave us"). The Song. Images. Complaint of the Dying Peasantry. The Church. Salem, Massachusetts. After a Hypothetical War. The Conqueror. An Island Tale. After 1984. The Strange Return. Three Tales. The Desola-tions. The Brothers. Dialogue ("Returning from the antipodes"). Sick Caliban. Penelope in Doubt. The Tower. Sonnet ("Do not mourn"). The Voices. Impersonal Calamity. The Last War. II (Unfinished Poems), The Poet. To the Forgotten Dead. Dialogue ("I never saw the world"). Petrol Shortage. Ballad of Everyman. Nightmare of Peace. III (Fragments of Poems), "There's nothing here." Dialogue ("I have heard you cry"). "The heart could never speak." "I see the image." "Our apprehensions give." "The refugees born for a land unknown." "And once I knew." Sunset. The Day before the Last Day. "I have been taught." Index of First Lines.

b. Second Edition. 1963

EDWIN MUIR | * | COLLECTED POEMS | FABER AND FABER | 24 RUSSELL SQUARE | LONDON

310 pp.   8 x 5¼ in.

(Identical with A29*a*, with these exceptions: p. [2] by the same author (eight titles); no frontispiece; p. [3] title; p. [4] Collected Poems 1921-1958 | first published in mcmlx | by Faber and Faber Limited | 24 Russell Square London W. C. 1 | Collected Poems mcmlxiii | Printed in Great Britain by | Western Printing Services Limited | All rights reserved | © This collection Willa Muir | 1960; pp. 7-8 re-set but not otherwise changed to accommodate on p. 8 Note on the Second Edition, as follows: For the second edition we have made a few amendments in two poems in the final section, "Dialogue" ("I have heard you cry") and "I have been taught," and some minor typographical changes elsewhere. A hitherto uncollected poem, "The Two Sisters," first published in 1956, has been added to the final section. We are indebted to Professors Peter Butter and Robert Hollander for suggesting some of these changes after a close study of the texts. W.M., J.C.H.)

Blue cloth boards; spine lettered in gold: EDWIN | MUIR | * | COL-LECTED | POEMS | FABER; all edges trimmed; end-papers. Rose-colored dust-jacket printed in black and white, publisher's advertisement on back cover.

Published January, 1964.   25s.

CONTENTS: As for A29*a*, with this addition: *Poems not previously collected:* I (Completed Poems), The Two Sisters.

A30   THE ESTATE OF POETRY   1962

a. First English Edition

* | THE ESTATE OF POETRY | EDWIN MUIR | 1962 | THE | HOGARTH PRESS | LONDON

xx, 118 pp.   8¼ x 5½ in.

One blank leaf; p. [i] * | The Estate of Poetry | The | Charles Eliot Norton | Lectures | 1955-1956; p. [ii] By the Same Author (eight titles); p. [iii] title; p. [iv] Published by | The Hogarth Press Ltd. | 42 William IV Street | London, W. C. 2 | Book design by David Ford | © Copyright 1962 by the President and Fellows of Harvard College | Printed in the United States of America; p. [v] contents; p. [vi] blank; pp. vii-xviii, Foreword by Archibald MacLeish; p. [xix] half-title; p. [xx] blank; pp. 1-110, text; p. [111] section title; p. [112] blank; pp. 113-115, A Note on Sources; p. [116] blank; pp. 117-118, Index of Names; two blank leaves.

Olive-green cloth boards; spine lettered in gold: * | THE | ESTATE | OF | POETRY | * | EDWIN | MUIR | * | THE | HOGARTH | PRESS; all edges trimmed; light olive end-papers with markings (to imitate vellum). White dust-jacket printed in red and flecked with tiny red and black markings, publisher's advertisement on back cover.

Published September, 1962. 16s.

CONTENTS: Foreword. The Natural Estate. Wordsworth: Return to the Sources. W. B. Yeats. Criticism and the Poet. Poetry and the Poet. The Public and the Poet. A Note on Sources. Index of Names.

b. First American Edition. 1962

* | THE ESTATE OF POETRY | EDWIN MUIR | HARVARD | UNIVERSITY | PRESS | CAMBRIDGE | 1962

xx, 118 pp. 8¼ x 5½ in.

(Identical with A30*a*, with these exceptions: p. [ii] blank; p. [iii] title; p. [iv] * | © Copyright 1962 by the President and Fellows of Harvard College | All rights reserved | Book design by David Ford | Library of Congress Catalog Card Number 62-9427 | Printed in the United States of America.)

Light olive paper boards with markings (to imitate vellum); spine lettered in gold on a green-brown rectangle: THE | ESTATE | OF | POETRY | * | MUIR, and at tail in green-brown ink: HARVARD; all edges trimmed; end-papers of same paper as that covering boards. Beige dust-jacket printed in shades of green and brown, publisher's advertisement on back cover.

Published 1962. $3.00

The imitation vellum paper of the English and American editions is identical in appearance.

CONTENTS: As for A30*a*.

ADDENDA

ADDENDA

ADDENDA

B. CONTRIBUTIONS TO BOOKS
(excluding selections reprinted in anthologies or other books)

B. CONTRIBUTIONS TO BOOKS

(excluding selections reprinted in anthologies or other books)

1930

B1 "Introductory Note" to Franz Kafka, *The Castle*. London. Pp. v-xii. *Cf.* D9.

1933

B2 "Introductory Note" to Franz Kafka, *The Great Wall of China*. London. Pp. vii-xvi. *Cf.* D16.

1936

B3 "Introductory Essay (IV)" to Robert Frost, *Selected Poems*. London. Pp. 29-35.

1940

B4 "Franz Kafka" [E.] in *A Franz Kafka Miscellany*. New York. Pp. 56-66.

1943

B5 *Poles in Uniform: Sketches of the Polish Army, Navy, and Air Force*, by Aleksander Żyw. Text by Edwin Muir. London. 128 pp. Muir's "text" consists of captions for Żyw's drawings.

1947

B6 "Poznámka k Franzi Kafkovi" in *Franz Kafka a Praha*. Prague. Pp. 35-39.

This essay was translated into Czech during Muir's residence in Prague, 1945-1948; it is reprinted in English in A23.

1948

B7   "A Tribute" in *T. S. Eliot, A Symposium*, compiled by Richard Marsh and Tambimuttu. London. Pp. 152-53.

1959

B8   "Translating from the German" in *On Translation*, ed. Reuben A. Brower. Cambridge, Mass. Pp. 93-94.

B9   "Preface" to *New Poets 1959*, ed. Edwin Muir. London. P. [5]. The poets selected by Muir to be included in this volume are Ian Crichton Smith, Karen Gershon, and Christopher Levenson.

ADDENDA

ADDENDA

C. CONTRIBUTIONS
TO PERIODICALS AND NEWSPAPERS

The nature of each of the following periodical contributions is designated by [P.] for poem(s), [E.] for essay, and [R.] for review. The abbreviation [R., incl. . . .] means that the review includes the work named, as well as others; if a title appears without this abbreviation it is the only work reviewed.

The following abbreviations have also been used:

Cal Mod Letters, Calendar of Modern Letters, later the *Calendar Quarterly*

Evening Post Lit Rev (NY), "Literary Review" of the New York *Evening Post*

Lit Digest, Literary Digest (New York)

Lond Mer, London Mercury

Mod Scot, Modern Scot

Nation, Nation and Athenæum

New S, New Statesman

SRL (NY), *Saturday Review of Literature* (New York)

Scots, Scotsman

Spec, Spectator

C. CONTRIBUTIONS
TO PERIODICALS AND NEWSPAPERS

C1   "The Epigram," *New Age*, XIII (May 29), 124.
     Edwin Muir's first published work is a short dialogue between
     "John" and "Tom" on the epigram which concludes: "Our writers
     are not serious enough even to *write* seriously . . . They can resist
     anything but an epigram."
     Numbers C1 through C126 (with the exception of the contribu-
     tions to the *Freeman* which were signed Edwin Muir) were pub-
     lished under the name "Edward Moore" or the initials "E. M."
C2   "Salutation" [P.], *New Age*, XIV (Nov. 6), 25-26.
C3   "A Chronicle of Woe" [P.], *New Age*, XIV (Dec. 11), 185.
C4   "A Question to My Love" [P.], *New Age*, XIV (Dec. 18), 197.
C5   "Address to Wage-Slaves" [P.], *New Age*, XIV (Dec. 18), 216-
     17.

1914

C6   "Utopia" [P.], *New Age*, XIV (April 16), 742.
C7   "Sleep's Betrayals" [P.], *New Age*, XV (May 7), 20.
C8   "To Present-day Critics; A Present-day Author to the Critics; The
     Same" [Epigrams], *New Age*, XV (July 2), 208.
C9   "To the War Poets" [P.], *New Age*, XV (Oct. 8), 553.
C10 "To the City Class" [P.], *New Age*, XV (Oct. 22), 601.
C11 "Metamorphosis" [P.], *New Age*, XVI (Nov. 5), 6.

1915

C12 "The Forsaken Princess" [P.], *New Age*, XVI (Feb. 25), 463.

1916

C13 "Epigrams: To Arnold Bennett; To the Same; To St. John G. Ervine," *New Age*, XVIII (March 23), 496.

C14 "Epigrams: To H. G. Wells; W. B. Yeats; James Stephens; John Masefield; Lascelles Abercrombie; Gerald Gould; W. H. Davies," *New Age*, XVIII (April 6), 544, 545.

C15 "Epigrams: John Masefield; James Stephens; Jack London; Sir Arthur Conan Doyle; Harold Begbie; Patrick MacGill; Maurice Hewlett; 'English Review'," *New Age*, XVIII (April 13), 568, 569.

C16 "Epigrams: Maurice Maeterlinck; George Bernard Shaw; John Galsworthy; Still More Epigrams," *New Age*, XVIII (April 20), 579, 595.

C17 "Odd Notes: Dangers of Genius; The Idealism of Love; These Advanced People; Middle Age's Betrayals; 'Words, Words, Words'*; Popularity; Realism; Modern Writing; Wilde; Art in Industry; Nietzsche; Fate and Mr. Wells; Strindberg; Psychologists; Dostoieffsky; The Chestertons,*" *New Age*, XIX (Oct. 12), 569-70. In spite of its title, this is the first entry in the "We Moderns" series, each article of which consists of paragraphs with separate titles. With the exception of the paragraphs marked by an asterisk, they are all reprinted in A1a.

C18 "We Moderns: The Modern Reader; The Intellectual Coquettes; The Advanced; Modern Realism; The Modern Tragic; The Novelists and The Artists; A Modern Problem; The Sex Novel; The Poet Speaks; The Good Fellows; Mr. G. K. Chesterton; Mr. G. K. Chesterton Again*; Whither?," *New Age*, XX (Nov. 16), 63-65.

C19 "We Moderns: Decadence; Decadence Again; Wilde and the Sensualists; Pater and the Aesthetes; The Average Man," *New Age*, XX (Dec. 14), 160-61.

1917

C20 "We Moderns: The Public; Original Sin; Again; Again; Equality; The Decay of Prophecy; The Question; The 'Restoration' of Christianity; The Dogmatists; The Ordinary and the Extraordinary; A Dilemma," *New Age*, XX (Jan. 18), 280-82.

C21 "We Moderns: Psychology of Style; Reader and Writer; Paradox;

The Precise; The 'New' Writers; Les Humbles; The Great Im-
moralists; Dostoieffsky; Art in Modern Society," *New Age*, XX
(Feb. 1), 327-28.

C22 "We Moderns: The Old Gods; The Old Poets; The Fall of Man;
Interpretations; The Use of Myth; Before the Fall; Beyond Origi-
nal Sin; The Eternal Blue-Stocking; Once More," *New Age*, XX
(Feb. 22), 401-02.

C23 "We Moderns: Majorities and Art; The Decay of Man; The Man
and the Hour; If Men were Equal; The Illusionists; The Lover to
the Artists; Origin of the Tragic; Tragedy and Comedy; Super-Art;
Literature and Literature; Literature as Praise," *New Age*, XX
(March 1), 423-24.

C24 "We Moderns: Creative Love; The God of Becoming; Where Man
is Innocent; A Criterion; Love at the Renaissance; Sympathy; A
Self-Evident Proposition; 'God is Love'; Myth," *New Age*, XX
(March 15), 470-71.

C25 "We Moderns: Love and Mr. Galsworthy; Mr. Thomas Hardy;
Mr. George Moore; Mr. Bernard Shaw; Mr. G. K. Chesterton;
Mr. H. G. Wells," *New Age*, XX (March 22), 496-98.

C26 "We Moderns: Psychology of the Humble; Against the Ostenta-
tiously Humble; The Pride of the Sterile; When Pride is Neces-
sary; Humility and the Artists; Love and Pride," *New Age*, XX
(April 5), 545-46.

C27 "We Moderns: Love and Becoming; Static Values; Utopias; 'Pri-
macy of Things'; Perfection; Goals; The Pessimists; The Other
Side; Sickness and Health; Love and Sympathy; The Humanitari-
ans; Love and the Virtues; Love and Danger," *New Age*, XX
(April 19), 592-93.

C28 "Letter to the Editor," *New Age*, XX (April 19), 598. An an-
swer to criticism of "We Moderns."

C29 "We Moderns: Tolerance of Artists; Climate; Sensibility; The Artists' Enemy; Uniformity; The Descent of the Artist; Immortality
of the Artist; Hostility of Thinkers; Artist and Philosopher; An
Evil; The Old Poet; The Platitude; Apropos the Cynic," *New Age*,
XXI (May 3), 14-15.

C30 "We Moderns: Compliments and Art; Leisure and Good Things;
Wanted: a History of Hurry; Leisure and Productiveness; Sex in
Literature; History of a Realist; The Only Course," *New Age*, XXI
(May 17), 63-64.

C31   "We Moderns: The Sin of Intellectualism; Pride and the Fall; The
      Good Conscience; The Other Side; History of the Dionysian;
      Tragic Affirmation," *New Age*, XXI (June 7), 138-39.

C32   "We Moderns: Conventions; 'Vitality'; What is Freedom?; Free-
      dom in the Dance; A Moral for Moderns; The Renaissance: A
      Thesis; The Unproductive Periods; 'Emancipation'; Genealogy of
      the Moderns," *New Age*, XXI (June 21), 182-83.

C33   "We Moderns: Duties of the Unproductive; Realism as a Symptom
      of Poverty; Domination of the Present; What is Modern?; How
      We Shall Be Known," *New Age*, XXI (July 5), 231-32.

C34   "We Moderns: Experimenting in Life; Criterions; Intellectual
      Prudence; A Dilemma; Decadence and Health; Dangers of the
      Spiritual; Again; God and Animal; Ultimate Pessimism," *New
      Age*, XXI (July 19), 269-70.

C35   "We Moderns: Praise?; Novelists by Habit; Going Down the
      Hill; The Average Man; Creator and Aesthete; Hypocrisy of
      Words; Love Poetry; The Twice Subtle; Mastery of One's
      Thoughts; Master and Servant; Multum in Parvo; The First and
      the Last; A Strange Failure; Humility in Pride," *New Age*, XXI
      (Aug. 2), 310-11.

C36   "We Moderns: Fellowship and Love; The Paradox; Moral Indig-
      nation; Morality and Love; Paradise Regained; Love and Knowl-
      edge; Proverb and Commentary; Bad Thoughts; Love and Sym-
      pathy; Love and the Senses; Love and Innocence; Love and the
      Fall; Love and Its Object; Freedom in Love; Love and the Sen-
      sualists; Free Will; Tragedy; Life and Love," *New Age*, XXI
      (Aug. 16), 349-50.

C37   "We Moderns: Life as Expression; 'Self-Expression'; Life as a
      Value; Hegel's Theory of Tragedy; Tragic Philosophy; Tragedy
      and Arguments; Morality and Happiness," *New Age*, XXI (Aug.
      30), 388-89.

C38   "We Moderns: End or Effect; Superiority; Beauty and Tragedy;
      Christian and Dionysian; Mastery and Tragedy; The Hidden Fac-
      ulty; The Other Side; Modern Art Themes; Encyclopædists; The
      Two Sides*; The Modern Devil; Nietzsche; Again; Sacrifices; Our
      Poverty; Finis," *New Age*, XXI (Sept. 13), 428-30.

C39   "Letter to the Editor," *New Age*, XXI (Oct. 4), 494-95.
      Muir's answer to criticism of "We Moderns."

1918

C40 "Earnest Trifles," *New Age*, XXII (Jan. 10), 217-18. Twenty-six
     short untitled paragraphs: the unprinted remains of "We Mod-
     erns"?

C41 "Caliban," *Guildsman*, No. 16 (March), pp. 4-5. A "playlet," a
     favorite literary form in this periodical. Although Muir was one
     of the founders and editors of the *Guildsman*, "Caliban" is his
     only signed work in the periodical and it bears his nom de plume,
     Edward Moore.

C42 "Recreations in Criticism" [E.], *New Age*, XXIII (Oct. 24), 411-
     12.

C43 "Recreations in Criticism" [E.], *New Age*, XXIV (Nov. 28), 58-
     59.

1919

C44 "Recreations in Criticism" [E.], *New Age*, XXIV (Jan. 2), 141-
     42.

C45 "Recreations in Criticism" [E. on Dostoyevsky], *New Age*, XXIV
     (Feb. 13), 243-45.

C46 "Recreations in Criticism" [E.], *New Age*, XXIV (April 24),
     412-13.

C47 "Mr. Thomas Hardy" [E.], *New Age*, XXV (May 8), 27-29.

C48 "Mr. George Bernard Shaw" [E.], *New Age*, XXV (July 10),
     184-86.

C49 "A Note on Mr. Conrad" [E.], *New S*, XIII (Sept. 13), 590-92.
     Cf. C54.

C50 "New Values" [E.], *New Age*, XXV (Sept. 18), 345-46.

C51 "New Values" [E.], *New Age*, XXV (Oct. 16), 409-10.

C52 "New Values" [E.], *New Age*, XXVI (Nov. 20), 39-40.

C53 "On Cleverness and Other Things" [Twenty-four aphorisms],
     English Review, XXIX (Dec.), 537-40.

1920

C54 "A Note on Mr. Conrad," *Living Age*, CCCIV (Jan. 10), 101-04.
     A reprint of C49.

C55 "New Values" [E.], *New Age*, XXVI (Feb. 5), 223-24.

C56 "Recreations in Criticism" [E.], *New Age*, XXVI (March 11), 306.

C57 "Recent Verse" [R.], *New Age*, XXVII (May 6), 11-13.

C58 "Wagner and Greek Tragedy" [R.], *Athenæum*, No. 4698 (May 14), p. 647.

None of Muir's reviews in the *Athenæum* were signed; those listed here (between C58 and C98) have been identified from the marked copies of the *Athenæum* now owned by the *New Statesman*.

C59 "Milton as Thinker" [R., Denis Saurat, *La Pensée de Milton*], *New Age*, XXVII (June 17), 107-08.

This review is almost identical with C60.

C60 "Foreign Literature" [R., Denis Saurat, *La Pensée de Milton*], *Athenæum*, No. 4704 (June 25), p. 843.

C61 "Recent Verse" [R.], *New Age*, XXVII (July 1), 139-40.

C62 "Recent Verse" [R., incl. Edith Sitwell, *Clowns' Houses*], *New Age*, XXVII (July 8), 154-55.

C63 "Recent Verse" [R., Ezra Pound, *Umbra*], *New Age*, XXVII (July 22), 186-87.

C64 "Les Futuristes Sont Passés" [R., F. T. Marinetti, *Les Mots en liberté futuristes*], *New Age*, XXVII (Aug. 19), 248-49.

C65 "The Nemesis of Sentimentalism" [E.], *New Age*, XXVII (Sept. 2), 269.

C66 "Who is Christ?" [E.], *New Age*, XXVII (Sept. 9), 281.

C67 "The Return to Nature" [E.], *New Age*, XXVII (Sept. 16), 293-94.

C68 "The Fall of Reason" [E.], *New Age*, XXVII (Sept. 23), 305.

C69 "Recreations in Criticism" [E.], *New Age*, XXVII (Oct. 14), 344-45.

C70 [R. in "Our Library Table" of *Iona* and *Vitalism and Scholasticism*], *Athenæum*, No. 4720 (Oct. 15), pp. 521-22.

The unsigned short reviews or notices in this weekly column were written by various reviewers (hence the specific identification) including Aldous Huxley, assistant editor of the *Athenæum*, who was in charge of "Our Library Table."

C71 [R. in "Our Library Table" of *Psychology of Dreams*], *Athenæum*, No. 4721 (Oct. 22), p. 553.

C72 [R. in "Our Library Table" of *About Many Things*], *Athenæum*, No. 4723 (Nov. 5), p. 618.

C73 "Our Generation," *New Age*, XXVIII (Nov. 11), 17. With the exception of the issues for Oct. 27, 1921, Feb. 9, 1922, and March 9, 1922, every number of the *New Age* to Sept. 28, 1922, (when Arthur Moore became editor) contains "Our Generation." There are ninety-six articles in all, each consisting of comments on topical events.

C74 [R. in "Our Library Table" of *Some Contemporary Novelists, A Defence of Liberty, Guild Socialism Re-Stated, One Man's Initiation*], *Athenæum*, No. 4724 (Nov. 12), pp. 653-54.

C75 "Plato and Indian Thought" [R., E. J. Urwick, *Message of Plato*], *Athenæum*, No. 4724 (Nov. 12), p. 651.

C76 "Recent Verse" [R., incl. Laurence Housman, *Heart of Peace*], *New Age*, XXVIII (Nov. 18), 32-33.

C77 [R. in "Our Library Table" of *N. D. Williams, Occultists and Mystics, ABC of Occultism*], *Athenæum*, No. 4725 (Nov. 19), p. 696.

C78 "Homage to Ruskin" [R.], *Athenæum*, No. 4725 (Nov. 19), p. 692.

C79 [R. in "Our Library Table" of *Natural History of Evil*], *Athenæum*, No. 4726 (Nov. 26), p. 729.

C80 [R. in "Our Library Table" of *The Fringe of Immortality*, and in "Novels in Brief" of *The Peony of Pao-Yu*], *Athenæum*, No. 4727 (Dec. 3), pp. 760, 763.

C81 "Reflections and Conjectures" [E.], *Freeman*, II (Dec. 8), 301-02.

C82 [R. in "Our Library Table" of *Old and New, Terrorism and Communism*], *Athenæum*, No. 4728 (Dec. 10), p. 811.

C83 [R. in "Our Library Table" of *Credit Power and Democracy, Natives of the Northern Territories, Direct Action, A Jacobean Letter-Writer, John Morley*], *Athenæum*, No. 4729 (Dec. 17), pp. 837-38.

C84 "Man and His Brother," *New Age*, XXVIII (Dec. 23), 96. A "prose-poem" description of the Super-Ego.

C85 "Dynamo-Psychism" [R., Gustave Geley, *From the Unconscious to the Conscious*], *Athenæum*, No. 4730 (Dec. 24), p. 867.

C86 [R. in "Our Library Table" of *Jewish View of Jesus, Kentucky Superstitions*], *Athenæum*, No. 4731 (Dec. 31), pp. 891-92.

C87 "Foreign Literature: Pascal" [R., *Les Lettres Provinciales*], *Athenæum*, No. 4731 (Dec. 31), p. 902.

1921

C88   [R. in "Our Library Table" of *Open Vision, Psychology and Mystical Experience*], *Athenæum*, No. 4732 (Jan. 7), pp. 17-18.

C89   [R., *Natural History Studies*], *Athenæum*, No. 4732 (Jan. 7), p. 20.

C90   "Recent Verse" [R., incl. Cloudesley Brereton, *Mystica et Lyrica*], *New Age*, XXVIII (Jan. 13), 127-28.
       Letter by Brereton and Muir's reply, XXVIII (Feb. 3), 168.

C91   [R. in "Our Library Table" of *Studies in Dreams, David Livingstone*], *Athenæum*, No. 4733 (Jan. 14), p. 44.

C92   [R. in "Our Library Table" of *House of Commons and Monarchy, Labour and Industry, Macedonia, Serbia and Europe*], *Athenæum*, No. 4734 (Jan. 21), p. 72.

C93   "Memory" [R., E. d'Eichthal, *Du Rôle de la Mémoire*], *Athenæum*, No. 4734 (Jan. 21), p. 82.

C94   "A Plea for Psychology in Literary Criticism" [E.], *Athenæum*, No. 4735 (Jan. 28), pp. 90-91.
       Letter of criticism by H. P. Collins, No. 4736 (Feb. 4), pp. 137-38; and Muir's reply, No. 4737 (Feb. 11), pp. 163-64.

C95   [R. in "Our Library Table" of *Naturalist in Himalaya*], *Athenæum*, No. 4736 (Feb. 4), p. 128.

C96   [R., M. de Montmorand, *Psychologie des Mystiques Catholiques Orthodoxes*], *Athenæum*, No. 4736 (Feb. 4), p. 139.

C97   [R. in "Our Library Table" of *Charles Chapin's Story, Psychology and Psychotherapy*], *Athenæum*, No. 4737 (Feb. 11), pp. 156-57.

C98   [R., *South African Mammals*], *Athenæum*, No. 4737 (Feb. 11), p. 159.

C99   "Reflections and Conjectures" [E.], *Freeman*, III (March 23), 38.

C100   "Recent Verse" [R.], *New Age*, XXVIII (March 31), 261-62.

C101   "Recent Verse" [R., incl. *Wheels 1920*], *New Age*, XXVIII (April 14), 284.

C102   "Recent Verse" [R., incl. Alexander Blok, *The Twelve*, trans. C. E. Bechhofer], *New Age*, XXIX (May 5), 8-9.

C103   "Recent Verse" [R., incl. Nancy Cunard, *Outlaws*], *New Age*, XXIX (May 26), 46-47.

C104   "The Reign of Superstition" [E.], *Freeman*, III (June 1), 273-75.

C105 "Recent Verse" [R., incl. Claude McKay, *Spring in New Hampshire*], *New Age*, XXIX (June 2), 57.

C106 "Recent Verse" [R.], *New Age*, XXIX (June 9), 69-70.

C107 "Recent Verse" [R., incl. E. H. W. Meyerstein, *Symphonies*], *New Age*, XXIX (June 16), 80-81.

C108 "The Affirmation of Suffering" [E.], *Freeman*, III (June 22), 347-48.

C109 "Recent Verse" [R.], *New Age*, XXIX (June 30), 104-05.

C110 "*L'Actuel:* An Unpublished Poem" [A study of Denis Saurat's poem with many quotations from it], *New Age*, XXIX (July 28), 153; (Aug. 25), 201-02; (Sept. 1), 213.

C111 "The Story of the Hungry Sheep" [E.], *Freeman*, IV (Sept. 14), 11-12.

C112 "Recent Verse" [R.], *New Age*, XXIX (Oct. 13), 286.

C113 "In Defence of New Truths" [E.], *Freeman*, IV (Oct. 19), 130-31.

C114 "New Values" [E.], *New Age*, XXIX (Oct. 27), 306-07.

C115 "Against the Wise" [E.], *Freeman*, IV (Nov. 16), 226-27.

C116 "Recent Verse" [R.], *New Age*, XXX (Nov. 17), 33-34.

C117 "Against Optimism and Pessimism" [E.], *Freeman*, IV (Dec. 7), 296-98.

C118 "Beyond the Absolute" [E.], *Freeman*, IV (Dec. 21), 345-46.

1922

C119 "Against Being Convinced" [E.], *Freeman*, IV (Jan. 11), 418-20.

C120 "Recent Verse" [R., incl. Gerald Gould, *Happy Tree;* and Richard Aldington, *Images, Images of Desire*], *New Age*, XXX (Jan. 12), 136-37.

C121 "The Truth About Art" [E.], *Freeman*, IV (Feb. 15), 537-39; V (March 15), 10-12.

C122 "Prague Letter" [E.], *Dial*, LXXII (April), 406-11.

C123 "Recent Verse" [R., incl. Amy Lowell, *Can Grande's Castle*], *New Age*, XXXI (May 4), 8-9.

C124 "Impressions of Prague" [E.], *Freeman*, V (May 10), 204-05.

C125 "De l'Amour" [E.], *Freeman*, V (May 17), 228-29.

C126 "Recent Verse" [R.], *New Age*, XXXI (May 25), 43-44.

C127 "Re-Birth" [P.], *New Age*, XXXI (June 8), 72.
This poem is Muir's first British publication under his own name.

With the exception of items C140 and C141 (published under the name "Edward Moore"), the following works were published under Muir's name, or (in a few cases) were signed by the initials "E. M.," or were unsigned.

C128 "Against Profundity" [E.], *Freeman*, V (June 14), 321-23.

C129 "Aphorisms," *Freeman*, V (June 21), 350-51.

C130 "On the Universe" [E.], *Freeman*, V (June 28), 368-69.

C131 "Ballad of Eternal Life" [P.], *New Age*, XXXI (July 6), 121-22.

C132 "Downfall of the Occident" [E. on Spengler], *New Age*, XXXI (July 20), 146-47.

C133 "Impressions of Prague" [E.], *Freeman*, V (Aug. 9), 510-12.

C134 "Aphorisms," *Freeman*, V (Aug. 23), 563-64.

C135 "Recent Verse" [R., Sacheverell Sitwell, *The Hundred and One Harlequins*], *New Age*, XXXI (Aug. 24), 211-12.
        Cf. C175.

C136 "A Note on Dostoievsky" [R., Janko Lavrin, *Dostoievsky and His Creation: A Psycho-Critical Study*], *Freeman*, VI (Sept. 13), 17-19.

C137 "Aphorisms," *Freeman*, VI (Sept. 20), 36-37.

C138 "Recent Verse" [R., incl. Ezra Pound, *Hugh Selwyn Mauberly*], *New Age*, XXXI (Oct. 5), 288.

C139 "Impressions of a People" [E.], *Freeman*, VI (Oct. 11), 108-09.

C140 "Labour's Statistical Boa-Constrictor" [E.], *New Age*, XXXI (Oct. 12), 297-98.

C141 "Recreations in Criticism" [E.], *New Age*, XXXI (Oct. 19), 317-18.

C142 "Causerie de Jeudi," *New Age*, XXXII (Nov. 9), 23-24.
        This is the first article in a series similar to "We Moderns," although the essays are less aphoristic in style. Toward the end of the run (there are 21 articles) they are frequently disguised reviews. The dates of publication are as follows: XXXII (Nov. 16), 38-39; (Nov. 23), 55-56; (Nov. 30), 71-72; (Dec. 7), 88-89; (Dec. 14), 103-04; (Dec. 28), 132-33; (Jan. 11, 1923), 164-65; (Jan. 18), 180-81; (Jan. 25), 198; (Feb. 8), 233-34; (Feb. 22), 270-71; (March 8), 307-08; (April 5), 367-68 [E. on Hoffman]; (April 12), 382-83 [E. on Hoffman continued]; (April 26), 413-14 [E. on E. O'Neill]; XXXIII (May 10), 22-24 [E. on Spengler]; (May 17), 41-42 [E. on W. H. Davies]; (July 12), 153-54 [sub-title, "Tolstoi in Love": R., *Tolstoi's Love Letters*]; (July 26), 181-82 [sub-title, "An Annual Anthology": R., *Best Poems 1922*,

ed. Thomas Moult]; (Aug. 16), 220-21 [sub-title, "The Essayists": R., *Essays of Today*].

C143 "A Note on Ibsen" [R., Janko Lavrin, *Ibsen and His Creation: A
Psycho-Critical Study*], *Freeman*, VI (Oct. 25), 162-64.

C144 "North and South" [E. in three parts], *Freeman*, VI (Nov. 15),
226-28; (Nov. 22), 249-51; (Nov. 29), 273-75.

1923

C145 "A Note on the Scottish Ballads" [E.], *Freeman*, VI (Jan. 17),
441-44.

C146 "Meditations" [aphorisms and notes], *Freeman*, VI (Feb. 7), 517-
18.

C147 "Meditations" [aphorisms and notes], *Freeman*, VI (March 7),
609-10.

C148 "A Note on Friedrich Nietzsche" [R., Janko Lavrin, *Nietzsche*],
Freeman, VII (March 14), 18-21.

C149 [R. in "Shorter Notices" of Philip Guedalla, *The Second Empire*],
Freeman, VII (March 21), 46-47.
This review and others in the "Shorter Notices" are signed "E. M."
Professor G. Thomas Tanselle, author of "Unsigned and Initialed
Contributions to *The Freeman*" in *Studies in Bibliography*, XVII
(1964), 153-75, has assured me that Muir was the author of all
pieces signed "E. M.," and further, that he most probably did not
write any of the unsigned pieces.

C150 "George Douglas" [E.], *Freeman*, VII (April 4), 80-83.
Letter by Abe Friedman, with correction of factual errors (April
25), 160.

C151 "The Larva" [P.], *New Age*, XXXII (April 19), 401.

C152 "From a Critic's Notebook" [four lengthy "notes"], *Freeman*, VII
(May 2), 183-84.

C153 "Robert Burns" [E.], *Freeman*, VII (May 9), 202-04.

C154 "A Forgotten Romantic" [E. on E. T. A. Hoffmann], *Freeman*,
VII (May 23), 250-52.
Cf. C213 and C142 (April 5, 1923).

C155 "To a Dream" [P.], *New Age*, XXXIII (May 24), 63.

C156 "A Minor Artist" [R., I. A. Bunin, *The Gentleman from San
Francisco and Other Stories*, trans. D. H. Lawrence, S. S. Koteli-
ansky, and Leonard Woolf], *Freeman*, VII (June 6), 309-10.
Cf. C181.

C157 "Recent Verse" [R., incl. Robert Graves, *Whipperginny*], *New Age*, XXXIII (June 7), 90-91.

C158 "The Literature of Idiosyncrasy" [R., Llewelyn Powys, *Ebony and Ivory*], *Freeman*, VII (June 13), 332.

C159 "Recent Verse" [R., incl. Edith Sitwell, *Bucolic Comedies*; and Walter de la Mare, *Thus Her Tale*], *New Age*, XXXIII (June 14), 103-04.

C160 "The Assault on Humanism" [E.], *Freeman*, VII (June 27), 369-71.

C161 [R. in "Shorter Notices" of F. L. Pattee, *The Development of the American Short Story*], *Freeman*, VII (June 27), 382.
Cf. C550.

C162 "Ballad of the Flood. Ballad of the Black Douglas. Ballad of the Monk" [P.], *Scottish Chapbook*, I (July), 339-47.

C163 "George Douglas," *Scottish Nation*, July 3. Cited by James Veitch, *George Douglas Brown*, p. 189. London, 1952.

C164 "The Drama of Transition" [R., Isaac Goldberg, *The Drama of Transition: Native and Exotic Playcraft*], *Freeman*, VII (July 4), 403-04.

C165 "Recent Verse" [R.], *New Age*, XXXIII (July 5), 147-48.

C166 [R. in "Shorter Notices" of Albert Guérard, *A Short History of the International Language Movement*], *Freeman*, VII (July 11), 430-31.

C167 [R. in "Shorter Notices" of C. T. Winchester, *An Old Castle and Other Essays*], *Freeman*, VII (July 18), 455.

C168 [R. in "Shorter Notices" of F. J. Harvey Darton, *The Soul of Dorset*], *Freeman*, VII (July 25), 477.

C169 "Chorus of the Newly Dead" [P.], *Scottish Chapbook*, II (Aug.), 2-8.
An early version of A4 with many textual differences. It includes one poem ("The Saint") omitted from A4 and omits two ("The Poet" and "The Mystic") found in A4. Only two choruses are given here.

C170 "A Note on Friedrich Hölderlin" [E.], *Freeman*, VII (Aug. 1), 488-90.

C171 [R. in "Shorter Notices" of Katherine Tynan, *The Wandering Years*], *Freeman*, VII (Aug. 1), 502.

C172 "A Great Writer" [R., Knut Hamsun, *Victoria*], *Freeman*, VII (Aug. 8), 522.

C173 [R. in "Shorter Notices" of *Problems of Modern Science: A Series of Lectures*, ed. A. Dendy], *Freeman*, VII (Aug. 8), 526.

C174 [R. in "Shorter Notices" of S. Miles, *Annotations*], *Freeman*, VII (Aug. 15), 551.

C175 "The Problem of Mr. Sitwell" [R., Sacheverell Sitwell, *The Hundred and One Harlequins*], *Freeman*, VII (Aug. 22), 571-72.
Cf. C135.

C176 "At Salzburg" [E. on the music festival], *New Age*, XXXIII (Aug. 23), 231-32.
Cf. 183.

C177 [R. in "Shorter Notices" of Lord Dunsany, *Plays of Near and Far* and *Plays of Gods and Men*], *Freeman*, VII (Aug. 29), 599.

C178 "An Unwilling Decadent" [R., Walter de la Mare, *The Riddle and Other Tales*], *Freeman*, VII (Sept. 5), 620-21.

C179 [R. in "Shorter Notices" of C. C. Josey, *The Social Philosophy of Instinct*], *Freeman*, VII (Sept. 5), 623.

C180 "Readers and Writers" [E. on E. M. Forster, *Pharos and Pharillon*], *New Age*, XXXIII (Sept. 6), 256-57.

C181 "Russian Soil" [R., I. A. Bunin, *The Village*, trans. I. F. Hapgood], *Freeman*, VIII (Sept. 12), 19-20.
Cf. C156.

C182 "Recent Verse" [R.], *New Age*, XXXIII (Sept. 13), 266-67.

C183 "At Salzburg" [E. on the music festival], *Freeman*, VIII (Sept. 19), 39-40.
Cf. C176.

C184 "Readers and Writers" [E. on *Talks with Tolstoi*], *New Age*, XXXIII (Sept. 20), 278.

C185 "Letters from Abroad: Italians, Americans and Others," *Freeman*, VIII (Sept. 26), 64-65.

C186 "A Genuine Essayist" [R., Aldous Huxley, *On the Margin*], *Freeman*, VIII (Oct. 3), 92-93.

C187 [R. in "Shorter Notices" of John Erskine, *The Literary Discipline*], *Freeman*, VIII (Oct. 3), 95.

C188 "Frank Wedekind" [R., Frank Wedekind, *Tragedies of Sex*, trans. S. A. Eliot, Jr.], *Freeman*, VIII (Oct. 10), 114-16.

C189 "Childhood" [P.], *Nation*, XXXIV (Oct. 13), 54.

C190 [R. in "Shorter Notices" of J. C. Squire, *American Poems and Others*], *Freeman*, VIII (Oct. 17), 143.

C191 "Readers and Writers" [E. on Romanticism and Classicism], *New Age*, XXXIII (Oct. 18), 329-30.

C192 "Hugo von Hofmannsthal" [E.], *Freeman*, VIII (Oct. 24), 152-54.

C193 [R. in "Shorter Notices" of Luigi Pirandello, *The Late Mattia Pascal*, trans. A. Livingston; F. Poulsen, *Travels and Sketches*, trans. anon.; and P. de Bacourt and J. W. Cunliffe, *French Literature During the Last Half-Century*], *Freeman*, VIII (Oct. 24), 167.

C194 "Sehnsucht in German Poetry" [E.], *Freeman*, VIII (Oct. 31), 178-80.

C195 [R. in "Shorter Notices" of John Drinkwater, *Robert E. Lee: A Play*], *Freeman*, VIII (Oct. 31), 191.

C196 "Recent Verse" [R.], *New Age*, XXXIV (Nov. 1), 8-9.

C197 "Swedish Tales" [R., *Modern Swedish Masterpieces*, trans. C. W. Stork], *Freeman*, VIII (Nov. 7), 213-14.

C198 [R. in "Shorter Notices" of *The Girdle of Aphrodite*, trans. F. A. Wright], *Freeman*, VIII (Nov. 7), 214-15.

C199 "The Art of Love" [R., Charles Vildrac, *A Book of Love*, trans. Witter Bynner], *Freeman*, VIII (Nov. 14), 237-38.

C200 "Readers and Writers" [R., C. M. Grieve, *Annals of the Five Senses*], *New Age*, XXXIV (Nov. 15), 32-33.

C201 "Recent Verse" [R., incl. Vachel Lindsay, *Collected Poems*], *New Age*, XXXIV (Nov. 29), 58.

C202 "Reverie" [P.], *Dial*, LXXV (Dec.), 534-35.

C203 "Childhood" [P.], *Living Age*, CCCXIX (Dec. 15), 528.

C204 "Edwin Muir and Francis George Scott: A Conversation," *Freeman*, VIII (Dec. 19), 348-51.

C205 "The Meaning of Romanticism" [E. in three parts], *Freeman*, VIII (Dec. 26), 368-70; (Jan. 9, 1924), 416-18; (Jan. 16, 1924), 443-44.

C206 "Readers and Writers" [E.], *New Age*, XXXIV (Dec. 27), 103-04.

1924

C207 "Poetry in Becoming" [R., D. H. Lawrence, *Birds, Beasts and Flowers*], *Freeman*, VIII (Jan. 2), 404-05.

C208 "Recent Verse" [R.], *New Age*, XXXIV (Jan. 3), 115-16.

C209 "Maya" [P.], *Nation*, XXXIV (Jan. 12), 545.

C210 [R. in "Shorter Notices" of H. Miles and R. Mortimer, *The Oxford Circus*], *Freeman*, VIII (Jan. 16), 455.

C211 "Readers and Writers" [E. on G. S. Marr, *Periodical Essayists of the Eighteenth Century*], *New Age*, XXXIV (Jan. 17), 139-40.

C212 "Miss Mansfield's Last Book" [R., Katherine Mansfield, *The Dove's Nest*], *Freeman*, VIII (Jan. 23), 477-78.

C213 "The Tales of Hoffmann" [R., E. T. A. Hoffman, *Weird Tales*, trans. J. T. Bealby], *Freeman*, VIII (Jan. 30), 498-99.
Cf. C154.

C214 [R. in "Shorter Notices" of Maurice Maeterlinck, *The Cloud That Lifted*, trans. F. M. Atkinson; and Gustav Wied, *2 × 2 = 5*, trans. E. Boyd and H. Kappel], *Freeman*, VIII (Jan. 30), 502-03.

C215 "Readers and Writers" [E. on works from Contact Publishing Company, Paris], *New Age*, XXXIV (Jan. 31), 164-65.

C216 "Childhood" [P.], *Dial*, LXXVI (Feb.), 122.

C217 "The Only Georgian" [R., W. H. Davies, *Collected Poems: Second Series*], *Freeman*, VIII (Feb. 13), 548-49.

C218 "October at Hellbrünn" [P.], *Nation*, XXXIV (Feb. 16), 701.

C219 "Hauptmann's Song of Songs" [R., Gerhart Hauptmann, *The Heretic of Soana*, trans. B. Q. Morgan], *Freeman*, VIII (Feb. 20), 571-72.

C220 "Irony and Pity" [R., Arthur Schnitzler, *Dr. Graesler*, trans. E. C. Slade], *Freeman*, VIII (Feb. 27), 596.
Cf. C251.

C221 "Prince Hempseed" [R., Stephen Hudson, *Prince Hempseed*], *Freeman*, VIII (March 5), 621-22.
Cf. C227, C267, C268, C325.

C222 "Recent Verse" [R.], *New Age*, XXXIV (March 6), 223.

C223 "Recent Verse" [R.], *New Age*, XXXIV (March 27), 260-61.

C224 "Grass" [P.], *Observer*, No. 6938 (May 18), p. 11.

C225 "Horses" [P.], *Nation*, XXXV (May 31), 293.
Reprinted in *Best Poems of 1924*, ed. Thomas Moult. London, 1925. "Horses" is Muir's first poem to be included in an anthology.

C226 "Novels of Mr. Hardy," *Evening Post Lit Rev* (NY), IV (June 7), 801-02.

C227 [R., Stephen Hudson, *Tony*], *Evening Post Lit Rev* (NY) IV (June 14), 819.
Cf. C221.

C228 "Ballad of Hector in Hades" [P.], *Adelphi*, II (Aug.), 242-43.

C229 "Women, Free for What?" [E.], *Nation* (NY), CXIX (Aug. 6), 140-42.

Reprinted in *Our Changing Morality*, ed. Freda Kirchwey. London, 1925.

C230 "Currents," *Evening Post Lit Rev* (NY), IV (Aug. 16), 961-62.

C231 "War and Nonsense" [R.], *Nation*, XXXV (Aug. 23), 647.

C232 "Old Style and New" [R.], *Nation*, XXXV (Aug. 30), 669-70.

C233 "Beauty and the Beast" [R., Edith Sitwell, *The Sleeping Beauty*], *SRL* (NY), I (Aug. 30), 76.

C234 "October at Hellbrünn" [P.], *Dial*, LXXVII (Sept.), 209.

C235 "Ballad of Hector in Hades" [P.], *Literary Digest*, LXXXII (Sept. 6), 38.

C236 "Remembrance" [P.], *Nation*, XXXV (Sept. 6), 692.

C237 "Juliet Looks at the World" [R., Jean Giradoux, *Juliette au Pays des Hommes*], *Nation*, XXXV (Sept. 13), 724.

C238 "The Marvellous Boy" [R., Edgell Rickword, *Rimbaud: The Boy and the Poet*], *SRL* (NY), I (Sept. 13), 109.

C239 "Mr. Lawrence Speeded Up" [R., D. H. Lawrence and M. L. Skinner *The Boy in the Bush*; and Willa Cather, *A Lost Lady*], *Nation*, XXXV (Sept. 20), 752.

C240 "Innocent and Otherwise" [R.], *Nation*, XXXV (Sept. 27), 782.

C241 "Raw Material and Finished Article" [R.], *Nation*, XXXVI (Oct. 4), 22, 24.

C242 "Mr. Forster Looks at India" [R., E. M. Forster, *A Passage to India*], *Nation* (NY), CXIX (Oct. 8), 379-80.

C243 "Remembrance" [P.], *Literary Digest*, LXXXIII (Oct. 11), 36.

C244 "Past and Present" [R., Gerald Gould, *The English Novel of Today*; and H. W. Hewett, *The Modern German Novel*], *Nation*, XXXVI (Oct. 18), 116, 118.

C245 "Verisimilitude" [R., Hugh Walpole, *The Old Ladies*; and J. C. Squire, *Grub Street Nights Entertainment*], *Nation*, XXXVI (Oct. 25), 158, 160.

C246 [R., John Eyton, *Expectancy*], *SRL* (NY), I (Nov. 1), 243.

C247 "Romance" [R., incl. John Masefield, *Sard Harker*; and Marcel Proust, *Within a Budding Grove*, trans. C. K. Scott Moncrieff], *Nation*, XXXVI (Nov. 8), 220.

C248 "Travellers" [R. of eight travel books], *Nation*, XXXVI (Nov. 8: supplement), 238, 240.

C249 "Realism and Fantasy" [R., Arnold Bennett, *Elsie and the Child*; and James Stephens, *In the Land of Youth*], *Nation*, XXXVI (Nov. 15), 270, 272.

C250 "Varieties of Realism" [R., John Galsworthy, *The White Monkey*;

Viola Meynell, *Young Mrs. Cruse*; and Victoria Sackville West, *Seducers in Ecuador*], *Nation*, XXXVI (Nov. 22), 302.

C251 "Exotic and Otherwise" [R., incl. Arthur Schnitzler, *Dr. Graesler*], *Nation*, XXXVI (Nov. 29), 334.
Cf. C220.

C252 "Recent Criticism" [R., Virginia Woolf, *Mr. Bennett and Mrs. Brown*; Roger Fry, *The Artist and Psycho-Analysis*; and T. S. Eliot, *Homage to Dryden*], *Nation*, XXXVI (Dec. 6), 370, 372.
Cf. C272.

C253 "A Note on *Ulysses*" [E.], *New Republic* (NY), XLI (Dec. 10: supplement), 4-6.

C254 "Fiction" [R., incl. Rose Macauley, *Orphan Island*], *Nation*, XXXVI (Dec. 13), 418.

C255 "Recent Fiction" [R.], *Nation*, XXXVI (Dec. 20), 447.

1925

C256 "The Poetry of Hölderlin" [E.], *SRL* (NY), I (Jan. 3), 434.

C257 "Plays of Mr. Galsworthy" [R.], *Nation*, XXXVI (Jan. 31), 616.

C258 "The Lost Land" [P.], *Dial*, LXXVIII (Feb.), 123-24.

C259 "D. H. Lawrence" [E.], *Nation* (NY), CXX (Feb. 11), 148-50.

C260 "China and Africa" [R., incl. Llewelyn Powys, *Black Laughter*], *Nation*, XXXVI (Feb. 14), 682-83.

C261 "Criticism Again" [R., S. T. Williams, *Studies in Victorian Literature*], *Nation*, XXXVI (Feb. 21), 719-20.

C262 "Fiction" [R., incl. Michael Sadleir, *The Noblest Frailty*], *Nation*, XXXVI (Feb. 28), 752-53.

C263 "Fiction" [R.], *Nation*, XXXVI (March 7), 780.

C264 "Fiction" [R., incl. Giovanni Verga, *Mastro-Don Gesualdo*, trans. D. H. Lawrence], *Nation*, XXXVI (March 14), 816.
Letter by Orlo Williams and Muir's reply, (March 28), 885.

C265 "Fiction" [R.], *Nation*, XXXVI (March 28), 892.

C266 "Letter from England," *SRL* (NY), I (April 4), 647.

C267 "Fiction" [R., incl. Stephen Hudson, *Myrtle*, and E. C. Mayne, *Inner Circle*], *Nation*, XXXVII (April 11), 51.
Cf. C268, C221.

C268 "An Artistic Triumph" [R., Stephen Hudson, *Myrtle*], *SRL* (NY), I (April 11), 661.
Cf. C267.

C269 "Edith Sitwell" [E.], *Nation* (NY), CXX (April 15), 426-27.

C270 "Fiction" [R.], *Nation*, XXXVII (April 18), 78-79.

C271 "Lytton Strachey" [E.], *Nation*, XXXVII (April 25), 102-04.

C272 "Mr. Eliot's Criticism" [R. T. S. Eliot, *Homage to Dryden*], *Cal Mod Letters*, I (May), 242-44.
Cf. C252.

C273 "Fiction" [R., incl. I. Compton-Burnett, *Pastors and Masters*], *Nation*, XXXVII (May 9), 179-80.

C274 "Fiction" [R., incl. Conrad Aiken, *Bring! Bring!* and Giovanni Verga, *Little Novels of Sicily*, trans. D. H. Lawrence], *Nation*, XXXVII (May 23), 240.
Cf. C282.

C275 "Fiction" [R., incl. D. H. Lawrence, *St. Mawr*], *Nation*, XXXVII (May 30), 270-71.

C276 "Arnold Bennett" [Fourth essay in the "Scrutinies" series], *Cal Mod Letters*, I (June), 290-96.
Reprinted in *Scrutinies*, ed. Edgell Rickword. London, 1928.

C277 "English Poets, and Others" [R., Edith Sitwell, *Troy Park*; John Crowe Ransom, *Grace After Meat*; I. A. Richards, *Principles of Literary Criticism*], *SRL* (NY), I (June 6), 807.

C278 "Lytton Strachey" [E.], *Nation* (NY), CXX (June 10), 658-60.

C279 "Fiction" [R., incl. Edith Wharton, *The Mother's Recompense*], *Nation*, XXXVII (June 13), 328.

C280 "Fiction" [R., incl. Robert Graves, *My Head! My Head!* and Michael Arlen, *Mayfair*], *Nation*, XXXVII (June 20), 372.

C281 "James Joyce: The Meaning of *Ulysses*" [E.], *Cal Mod Letters*, I (July), 347-55.

C282 [R., Conrad Aiken, *Bring! Bring!*], *Criterion*, III (July), 583-84.
Cf. C274.

C283 "D. H. Lawrence" [E.], *Nation*, XXXVII (July 4), 425-27.
Correspondence, (Aug. 21), 581-82; Muir's reply, (Sept. 11), 669.

C284 "Fiction" [R., incl. Sherwood Anderson, *A Story Teller's Story*], *Nation*, XXXVII (July 11), 462-63.

C285 "A Letter from England," *SRL* (NY), I (July 25), 934.

C286 [R., Mary Butts, *Ashe of Rings*], *Cal Mod Letters*, I (Aug.), 476-78.
Reprinted in *Towards Standards of Criticism*, ed. F. R. Leavis. London, 1933.

C287 "Joie de Vivre" [R., Felix Timmermans, *Pallieter*], *Dial*, LXXIX (Aug.), 118-20.

C288 "Fiction" [R., incl. *Flying Osip: Stories of New Russia*, trans. L. Friedland and J. Piroshnikoff], *Nation*, XXXVII (Aug. 1), 546-47.

C289 "T. S. Eliot" [E.], *Nation* (NY), CXXI (Aug. 5), 162-64.

C290 "Fiction" [R., incl. Edward Sackville West, *Piano Quintet*], *Nation*, XXXVII (Aug. 15), 600.

C291 "T. S. Eliot" [E.], *Nation*, XXXVII (Aug. 29), 644-46.

C292 [R., George Santayana, *Dialogues in Limbo*], *Cal Mod Letters*, II (Sept.), 63-65.

C293 "Czech Fiction" [R., *Selected Czech Tales*, ed. Busch and Pick], *Nation*, XXXVII (Sept. 12), 708-09.

C294 "Fiction" [R., incl. Violet Hunt, *More Tales of the Uneasy*], *Nation*, XXXVII (Sept. 26), 767.

C295 "The Zeit Geist" [E.], *Cal Mod Letters*, II (Oct.), 112-18.

C296 "Proust in English" [R., Marcel Proust, *The Guermantes Way*, trans. C. K. Scott Moncrieff], *Nation*, XXXVIII (Oct. 3), 20.

C297 "James Joyce" [E.], *Nation* (NY), CXXI (Oct. 14), 421-23.

C298 "Fiction" [R.], *Nation*, XXXVIII (Oct. 17), 119.

C299 "Scottish Renaissance," *SRL* (NY), II (Oct. 31), 259. Survey of the contemporary movement, with special notice of *Sangschaw* by "Hugh MacDiarmid."

C300 "Fiction" [R., incl. Ford Madox Ford, *No More Parades*], *Nation*, XXXVIII (Oct. 31), 186.

C301 "Fiction" [R.], *Nation*, XXXVIII (Nov. 14), 262.

C302 "British Books: Autumn," *Nation* (NY), CXXI (Nov. 18), 577. A survey of new books.

C303 "The Zeitgeist" [E.], *Living Age*, CCCXXVII (Nov. 28), 459-63.

C304 "Fiction" [R., incl. Percy Lubbock, *The Region Cloud*], *Nation*, XXXVIII (Nov. 28), 324, 326.

C305 "Poems from *Chorus of the Newly Dead*" ["The Coward; The Harlot; The Mystic"], *Cal Mod Letters*, II (Dec.), 244-47.

C306 "Stephen Hudson" [E.], *Nation* (NY), CXXI (Dec. 9), 661-62.

C307 "Fiction" [R., incl. Willa Cather, *The Professor's House;* and Karel Capek, *Krakatit*, trans. L. Hyde], *Nation*, XXXVIII (Dec. 19), 440.

1926

C308 "The Present State of Poetry" [E.], *Cal Mod Letters*, II (Jan.), 322-31.

C309 "Fiction" [R.], *Nation*, XXXVIII (Jan. 30), 620.

C310 "Aldous Huxley" [E.], *Nation* (NY), CXXII (Feb. 10), 144-45.

C311 "Fiction" [R., incl. D. H. Lawrence, *The Plumed Serpent*], *Nation*, XXXVIII (Feb. 20), 719-20.

C312 "Aldous Huxley" [E.], *Nation*, XXXVIII (Feb. 27), 743-44.

C313 "The Present State of Poetry" [E.], *Living Age*, CCCXXVIII (March 6), 526-32.

C314 "Fiction" [R., incl. Richard Hughes, *A Moment of Time*], *Nation*, XXXVIII (March 6), 782.

C315 "Fiction" [R.], *Nation*, XXXVIII (March 13), 816.

C316 "Fiction" [R., incl. Lady Murasaki, *The Sacred Tree*, trans. Arthur Waley], *Nation*, XXXVIII (March 27), 900, 902.

C317 "Virginia Woolf" [E.], *Nation*, XXXIX (April 17), 70-72.

C318 "Friedrich Hölderlin" [E.], *Adelphi*, III (May), 799-807.
Contains a number of lines of Hölderlin's verse translated by Muir.

C319 "Romanticism" [R., A. E. Powell, *Romantic Theory of Poetry*], *Nation*, XXXIX (May 1), 132-33.

C320 "Two Views of French Literature" [R., incl. Richard Aldington, *French Studies and Reviews*], *Nation*, XXXIX (June 5), 253.

C321 "Fiction" [R., incl. Aldous Huxley, *Two or Three Graces;* and Anita Loos, *Gentlemen Prefer Blondes*], *Nation*, XXXIX (June 12), 284, 286.

C322 "Herman Melville" [R., John Freeman, *Herman Melville*], *Nation*, XXXIX (June 19), 324.

C323 "Virginia Woolf" [E.], *Nation* (NY), CXXII (June 30), 721-23.

C324 [R., Graham Wallas, *The Art of Thought*], *Calendar Qtly*, III (July), 160-61.

C325 "Fiction" [R., incl. Stephen Hudson, *Richard, Myrtle and I*; and novels by Pío Baroja], *Nation*, XXXIX (July 10), 420-21.
Cf. C221.

C326 "The Modern Novel" [R., E. A. Drew, *The Modern Novel*], *Nation*, XXXIX (July 17), 448.

C327 "Fiction" [R., incl. Sinclair Lewis, *Mantrap*], *Nation*, XXXIX (July 31), 506-07.

C328 "Contemporary Russian Literature" [R., D. S. Mirsky, *Contemporary Russian Literature*], *Nation*, XXXIX (Aug. 7), 533.

C329 "Mr. Robert Graves" [E.], *Nation*, XXXIX (Aug. 14), 554-55.

C330 "Fiction" [R.], *Nation*, XXXIX (Aug. 28), 615.

C331 "Romanticism" [R., Lascelles Abercrombie, *Romanticism*], *Nation*, XXXIX (Sept. 4), 644.

C332   "Robert Graves" [E.], *Nation* (NY), CXXIII (Sept. 8), 217-19.

C333   "Plots" [R., N. I. Sholto-Douglas, *Synopses of English Fiction*], *Nation*, XXXIX (Sept. 11), 675.

C334   "Miss Edith Sitwell" [E.], *Nation*, XXXIX (Sept. 18), 698-700.

C335   "Maupassant" [R., R. H. Sherard, *Life, Work and Evil Fate of Maupassant*], *Nation*, XXXIX (Sept. 18), 704.

C336   "Fiction" [R., incl. Rudyard Kipling, *Debits and Credits*; W. S. Maugham, *The Casuarina Tree*; and Edward Sackville West, *The Ruin*], *Nation*, XL (Oct. 9), 28, 30.

C337   "Fiction" [R., incl. Theodore Dreiser, *An American Tragedy*], *Nation*, XL (Oct. 16), 88-89.

C338   "Fiction" [R., incl. Osbert Sitwell, *Before the Bombardment;* and Ford Madox Ford, *A Man Could Stand Up*], *Nation*, XL (Oct. 23), 116.

C339   "The Open Conspiracy" [R., novels by H. G. Wells], *Nation*, XL (Nov. 6), 185-86.

C340   "Translations and Tomfooleries" [R., G. B. Shaw, *Translations and Tomfooleries*], *Nation*, XL (Dec. 4), 341-42.

C341   "A Study of Swinburne" [R., T. E. Welby, *A Study of Swinburne*], *Nation*, XL (Dec. 11), 390.

1927

C342   "Henry James" [R., Pelham Edgar, *Henry James*], *Nation*, XL (Jan. 1), 483.

C343   "Verse" [R., incl. "Hugh MacDiarmid," *A Drunk Man Looks at the Thistle*], *Nation*, XL (Jan. 22), 568.

C344   "Enigmas" [R., novels by Eden Phillpotts], *Nation*, XL (Feb. 12), 666, 668.

C345   "Fiction" [R., incl. David Garnett, *Go She Must*; and Luigi Pirandello, *Shoot!*], *Nation*, XL (Feb. 19), 700-01.

C346   "Fiction" [R., incl. J. B. Priestley, *Adam in Moonshine*], *Nation*, XL (Feb. 26), 728, 730.

C347   "Fiction" [R., incl. Elinor Wylie, *Mortal Image*; and Beverley Nichols, *Crazy Pavements*], *Nation*, XL (March 12), 802.

C348   "Fiction" [R., incl. J. D. Beresford, *The Tapestry*; and Joseph Hergesheimer, *Tampico*], *Nation*, XL (March 26), 898, 900.

C349   "Fiction" [R.], *Nation*, XLI (April 9), 19-20.

C350   "Fiction" [R., incl. Sinclair Lewis, *Elmer Gantry*], *Nation*, XLI (April 23), 85.

C351 "Fiction" [R.], *Nation*, XLI (May 7), 154.

C352 "Fiction" [R.], *Nation*, XLI (May 21), 220.

C353 "Fiction" [R., incl. Theodore Dreiser, *Sister Carrie*], *Nation*, XLI (June 4), 309-10.

C354 "Fiction" [R., incl. Conrad Aiken, *Blue Voyage*; Jean Giradoux, *Bella*, trans. J. Scanlan; and Gertrude Stein, *Three Lives*], *Nation*, XLI (June 18), 373-74.

C355 [R., Ramon Fernandez, *Messages*, trans. M. Belgion], *Calendar Qtly*, IV (July), 161-64.

C356 "Fiction" [R., incl. Virginia Woolf, *To the Lighthouse*; and Ernest Hemingway, *Fiesta*], *Nation*, XLI (July 2), 450, 452.

C357 "Fiction" [R., incl. Arnold Bennett, *The Woman Who Stole Everything*], *Nation*, XLI (July 16), 519-20.

C358 "The Trance" [P.], *Saturday Review*, CXLIV (July 23), 130.

C359 "A Life of Thackeray" [R., Lewis Melville, *Thackeray*], *Nation*, XLII (Oct. 8), 26.

C360 "Fiction" [R.], *Nation*, XLII (Oct. 15), 87-88.

C361 "Fiction" [R., incl. Theodore Dreiser, *The Financier*], *Nation*, XLII (Oct. 22), 120, 122.

C362 "Fiction" [R., incl. Hugh Kingsmill, *Blondel*], *Nation*, XLII (Nov. 5), 190, 192.

C363 "Fiction" [R., incl. Dorothy Richardson, *Oberland*], *Nation* XLII (Nov. 19), 284, 286.

C364 "Past and Present" [E.], *Atlantic Monthly*, CXL (Dec.), 776-81.

C365 "Fiction" [R., incl. Upton Sinclair, *Love's Pilgrimage*; and Thornton Wilder, *The Bridge of San Luis Rey*], *Nation*, XLII (Dec. 10), 402, 404.

C366 "Fiction" [R., incl. T. F. Powys, *Mr. Weston's Good Wine*; Wyndham Lewis, *The Wild Body*; Willa Cather, *Death Comes For The Archbishop*], *Nation*, XLII (Dec. 24), 488-89.

1928

C367 "The Trance" [P.], *Bookman* (NY), LXVI (Jan.), 499.

C368 "Don Quixote Interpreted" [R., M. Unamuno, *Don Quixote*], *Nation*, XLII (Jan. 14), 570-71.

C369 "Essays" [R.], *Nation*, XLII (Jan. 28), 656, 658.

C370 "Fiction" [R., incl. J. B. Cabell, *Something About Eve*; and Julian Green, *Avarice House*], *Nation*, XLII (Feb. 4), 689-90.

C371 "Fiction" [R., incl. Ford Madox Ford, *The Last Post*], *Nation*, XLII (Feb. 18), 752-53.

C372 "Fiction" [R., incl. J. B. Cabell, *Domnei*], *Nation*, XLII (Feb. 25), 784.

C373 "A German Estimate of Dostoyevsky" [R., J. Maier-Graefe, *Dostoyevsky*, trans. H. H. Marks], *Nation*, XLII (March 31), 972, 974.

C374 "Past and Present" [R., Sherard Vines, *Movements in Modern English Poetry and Prose*; and Margharita Widdows, *English Literature*], *Nation*, XLIII (April 14), 49.

C375 "George Eliot" [R., Arthur Paterson, *George Eliot's Family Life and Letters*], *Nation*, XLIII (April 28), 111.

C376 "Tristram Crazed" [P.], *Atlantic Monthly*, CXLI (May), 627-28.

C377 "The Eternal Moment" [R., E. M. Forster, *The Eternal Moment*], *Nation*, XLIII (May 12), 184.

C378 "Essays" [R., incl. Arnold Bennett, *The Savour of Life*; and J. B. Priestley, *Apes and Angels*], *Nation*, XLIII (May 26), 256.

C379 "The World of the Novel" [E.], *Atlantic Monthly*, CXLII (Nov.), 643-51.

C380 "Tristram Crazed" [P.], *New Adelphi*, II (Dec.), 100-01.

1929

C381 "Tristram Crazed" [P.], *Literary Digest*, C (Feb. 2), 27.

C382 "The Stationary Journey" [P.], *Bookman* (NY), LXIX (June), 355-56.
Reprinted in *Living Scottish Poets*, ed. C. M. Grieve. London, 1931.

C383 "Transmutation" [P.], *Bookman* (NY), LXX (Nov.), 233.

1930

C384 "Parallels" [E.], *Mod Scot*, I (Spring), 6-10.

C385 "Parallels" [E.], *New Freeman*, I (April 12), 106-08.

C386 "An English Letter," *New Freeman*, I (June, 18), 325-27.

C387 "Generations" [E.], *New Freeman*, II (Oct. 8), 85-87.

C388 "A Note on Franz Kafka," *Bookman* (NY), LXXII (Nov.), 235-41.

C389 "Reynard the Fox" [E.], *New S*, XXXVI (Nov. 1), 112-13.

C390 "A Note on Hans Carossa," *Bookman* (NY), LXXII (Dec.), 404-08.

C391 "Reynard the Fox" [E.], *New Freeman*, II (Dec. 10), 300, 302.

1931

C392 "The Fall" [P.], *Mod Scot*, I (Jan.), 10-11.

C393 "An English Letter," *New Freeman*, II (Jan. 28), 473-74.

C394 "Laurence Sterne" [E.], *Bookman* (NY), LXXIII (March), 1-5.

C395 "The Scottish Renaissance" [E.], *New Freeman*, II (March 11), 612-14.

C396 "After the Fall" [P.], *Bookman* (NY), LXXIII (April), 123-24.

C397 "After the Fall" [P.], *Criterion*, X (April), 421-23.

C398 [R., "Hugh MacDiarmid," *To Circumjack Cencrastus*], *Criterion*, X (April), 516-20.

C399 "The Novel" [E.], *New Freeman*, III (May 6), 178-80.

C400 "Robert Louis Stevenson" [E.], *Bookman* (NY), LXXIV (Sept.), 55-60.

C401 "Robert Louis Stevenson" [E.], *Mod Scot*, II (Oct.), 196-204.

C402 "Virginia Woolf" [E.], *Bookman* (NY), LXXIV (Dec.), 362-67.

1932

C403 "A Death (A Chapter from a Novel)," *Mod Scot*, II (Jan.), 270-76.
Chapter 22 of *Poor Tom*.

C404 "Chapter from a Novel: *Warum? Wofür? Wodurch? Wohin? Wo? Wie?*—Nietzsche," *Mod Scot,* III (April), 9-13.
Chapter 19 of *Poor Tom*.

C405 "Aldous Huxley" [R., *Rotunda: Selections from the Works of Aldous Huxley*], *New English Weekly*, I (July 14), 309-10.

C406 "A New Scottish Novelist" [R., Fioun MacColla, *The Albannach*], *Mod Scot*, III (Aug.), 166-67.

C407 "Hermann Broch" [E.], *Mod Scot*, III (Aug.), 103-110.
Preceded by "The Proposal: Chapter from a Novel [*The Sleepwalkers*] by Hermann Broch . . . translated by Edwin and Willa Muir, to be published in the autumn by Messrs. Martin Secker" (p. 98).

C408 "Scott and Tradition" [E.], *Mod Scot*, III (Aug.), 118-20.

C409 "Best Sellers of Yesterday: VI. William Black" [E.], *Listener*, VIII
(Sept. 7), 344-45.
Muir's first contribution to the *Listener*. Cf. C418.

C410 "Sir Walter Scott" [E.], *Spec*, No. 5439 (Sept. 24), pp. 364-65.
Muir's first contribution to the *Spectator*.

C411 [Introductory paragraph to Franz Kafka, "Aphorisms," trans.
Willa and Edwin Muir], *Mod Scot*, III (Oct.), 202.

C412 "The Main Problem," *Free Man*, I (Oct. 15), 5.

C413 "Hermann Broch" [E.], *Bookman* (NY), LXXV (Nov.), 664-68.

C414 "The Forty-Five" [R., Clennell Wilkinson, *Bonnie Prince Char-
lie*], *Spec*, No. 5445 (Nov. 4), p. 634.

C415 "Scotland's Problems" [R., D. C. Thomson, *Scotland in Quest of
Her Youth*], *Spec*, No. 5447 (Nov. 18), pp. 709, 711.

C416 "Interregnum" [P.], *Spec*, No. 5450 (Dec. 9), p. 827.

C417 "Scots Translators" [R., Alexander Gray, *Arrows: German Ballads
and Folk Songs Attempted in Scots*; and Margaret Winefride Simp-
son, *The Amber Lute: Poems from the French*], *Spec*, No. 5433
(Dec. 30), pp. 926-27.

1933

C418 "New Novels" [R.], *Listener*, IX (Jan. 25), 152.
Muir's first review for the *Listener*. Cf. 971.

C419 "Interregnum" [P.], *Literary Digest*, CXV (Jan. 28), 42.

C420 "New Short Stories" [R., incl. D. H. Lawrence, *The Lovely Lady*;
and James Joyce, *Two Tales of Shem and Shaun*], *Listener*, IX
(Feb. 8), 232.

C421 "The Functionless of Scotland," *Free Man*, II (Feb. 11), 6.

C422 "New Novels" [R.], *Listener*, IX (March 8), 392.

C423 "Readers and Writers" [R., first issue *New Verse*], *New English
Weekly*, II (March 9), 494-95.

C424 "New Novels" [R.], *Listener*, IX (March 22), 472.

C425 "Two Poets" [R., Roy Campbell, *Flowering Reeds*; William Montgomerie, *Via: Poems*], *Mod Scot*, IV (April), 67-70.

C426 "New Novels" [R., incl. William March, *Company K*], *Listener*,
IX (April 5), 556.

C427 "Literary Combat" [R.], *Spec*, No. 5468 (April 14), p. 538.

C428 "New Novels" [R.], *Listener*, IX (April 19), 644.

C429 "Modern German Literature" [R., A. Eloesser, *Modern German
Literature*], *Spec*, No. 5469 (April 21), pp. 574-75.

C430 "New Novels" [R.], *Listener*, IX (May 3), 723.

C431 "New Novels" [R.], *Listener*, IX (May 17), 803.

C432 "Autobiography" [P.], *Spec*, No. 5474 (May 26), p. 764.

C433 "Mary, Queen of Scots" [R., Eric Linklater, *Mary, Queen of Scots*], *Spec*, No. 5474 (May 26), p. 766.

C434 "New Novels" [R.], *Listener*, IX (May 31), 884.

C435 "New Novels" [R.], *Listener*, IX (June 14), 961.

C436 "New Novels" [R.], *Listener*, IX (June 28), 1044.

C437 "In the Wilderness" [P.], *Mod Scot*, IV (July), 138-40.

C438 "New Novels" [R.], *Listener*, X (July 12), 76.

C439 "New Novels" [R.], *Listener*, X (July 26), 147.

C440 "Scottish Literature" [R., A. M. McKenzie, *Historical Survey of Scottish Literature*], *New S*, VI (Aug. 5), 164.

C441 "New Novels" [R.], *Listener*, X (Aug. 9), 222.

C442 "The Riders" [P.], *Listener*, X (Aug. 16), 255.
Reprinted in *The Year's Poetry*, ed. D. K. Roberts, *et al*. London, 1934; also in *Poems of Tomorrow*, ed. Janet Adam Smith. London, 1935.

C443 "New Novels" [R., incl. I. Compton-Burnett, *More Women Than Men*], *Listener*, X (Aug. 23), 294.

C444 "Robert Henryson" [R., *Poems and Fables of Robert Henryson*, ed. H. H. Wood], *Spec*, No. 5488 (Sept. 1), p. 290.

C445 "New Novels" [R.], *Listener*, X (Sept. 6), 368.

C446 "New Novels" [R.], *Listener*, X (Sept. 20), 440.

C447 "New Novels" [R., incl. William Faulkner, *These Thirteen*], *Listener*, X (Oct. 4), 519.

C448 "New Novels" [R.], *Listener*, X (Oct. 18), 604.

C449 "Balderdash" [R., Oswald Spengler, *Jahre der Entscheidung*], *Spec*, No. 5495 (Oct. 20), p. 531.

C450 "New Novels" [R.], *Listener*, X (Nov. 1), 684.

C451 "New Novels" [R., incl. George Barker, *Alanna Autumnal*], *Listener*, X (Nov. 8), 728.

C452 "The Use of Poetry" [R., T. S. Eliot, *The Use of Poetry*], *Spec*, No. 5499 (Nov. 17), p. 703.

C453 "New Novels" [R.], *Listener*, X (Nov. 22), 807.

C454 "Three Important Books" [R.], *Bookman*, LXXXV (Dec.), 139-41.

C455 "The Threefold Time" [P.], *New Verse*, No. 6 (Dec.), pp. 3-4.

C456 "New Novels" [R.], *Listener*, X (Dec. 6), 887.

C457 "Popularization" [R., *Edinburgh Essays*, preface by H. J. C. Grierson], *Spec*, No. 5503 (Dec. 15), p. 907.
This highly critical review is unsigned and has been identified as Muir's from the *Spectator* MSS book.

C458 "New Novels" [R., incl. Lion Feuchtwanger, *The Oppermanns*], *Listener*, X (Dec. 20), 968.

C459 "The Dilemma" [P.], *Spec*, No. 5504 (Dec. 22), p. 932.

1934

C460 "The Decline of the Novel" [E.], *Mod Scot*, IV (Jan.), 284-90.

C461 "New Novels" [R., incl. Eric Linklater, *Magnus Merriman*], *Listener*, XI (Jan. 10), 80.

C462 "New Novels" [R.], *Listener*, XI (Jan. 24), 171.

C463 "New Novels" [R.], *Listener*, XI (Feb. 7), 256.

C464 "New Novels" [R., incl. Graham Greene, *It's a Battlefield*; Ernest Hemingway, *Winner Take Nothing*], *Listener*, XI (Feb. 21), 340.

C465 "New Novels" [R.], *Listener*, XI (March 7), 424.

C466 "Heraldry" [P.], *Spec*, No. 5515 (March 9), p. 375.
Reprinted in *The Year's Poetry*, ed. D. K. Roberts, *et al.* London, 1934.

C467 "Mr. Eliot on Evil" [R., T. S. Eliot, *After Strange Gods*], *Spec*, No. 5515 (March 9), pp. 378-79.

C468 "New Short Stories" [R.], *Listener*, XI (March 21), 508.

C469 "Prosperous Orkneys" [E.], *Spec*, No. 5518 (March 30), pp. 300-01.

C470 "New Novels" [R., incl. *Tales of D. H. Lawrence*], *Listener*, XI (April 4), 596.

C471 "New Novels" [R., incl. M. A. Sholokhov, *And Quiet Flows the Don*], *Listener*, XI (April 18), 680.

C472 "Scottish Poetry" [R., *A Book of Scottish Verse*, ed. R. L. Mackie], *Spec*, No. 5521 (April 20), p. 625.

C473 "Bolshevism and Calvinism" [E.], *European Qtly*, I (May), 3-11.

C474 "New Novels" [R.], *Listener*, XI (May 2), 768.

C475 "Poetic Diction" [R., Ronald Bottrall, *Festivals of Fire*], *Spec*, No. 5524 (May 11), pp. 746, 748.

C476 "New Novels" [R.], *Listener*, XI (May 16), 852.

C477 "Literature in Scotland," *Spec*, No. 5526 (May 25), p. 823.
A survey of the Scottish Renaissance.

C478 "Scottish Poetry" [R., William Montgomerie, *Squared Circle*; and Ronald Macfie, *Love Poems*], *Spec*, No. 5526 (May 25), p. 828. This rather critical review is signed "E. M."

C479 "New Novels" [R.], *Listener*, XI (May 30), 936.

C480 "New Novels" [R., incl. Thomas Mann, *Tales of Jacob*], *Listener*, XI (June 13), 1020.

C481 "Bolshevism and Calvinism" [E.], *New English Weekly*, V (June 21), 224-26. Correspondence, (July 12), 296-97; and Muir's reply, (Sept. 27), 463-64.

C482 "New Short Stories" [R., incl. Samuel Beckett, *More Pricks Than Kicks*], *Listener*, XII (July 4), 42.

C483 "New Novels" [R.], *Listener*, XII (July 18), 128.

C484 "The Contemporary Novel" [E.], *European Qtly*, I (Aug.), 70-76. *Cf.* C822.

C485 "New Novels" [R.], *Listener*, XII (Aug. 1), 216.

C486 "New Novels" [R.], *Listener*, XII (Aug. 22), 342.

C487 "Contemporary Scottish Poetry" [E.], *Bookman*, LXXXVI (Sept.), 282-83.

C488 "New Novels" [R.], *Listener*, XII (Sept. 12), 464.

C489 "New Novels" [R., incl. Evelyn Waugh, *A Handful of Dust*], *Listener*, XII (Sept. 19), 506.

C490 "What Is the Short Story?" [E.], *Lovat Dickson's Magazine*, III (Oct.), 463.

C491 "The Stronghold" [P.], *Mod Scot*, V (Oct.), 159.

C492 [Six answers to questions about poetry], *New Verse*, No. 11 (Oct.), p. 17.

C493 "New Novels" [R.], *Listener*, XII (Oct. 3), 590.

C494 "Prose and Conversation" [R., Bonamy Dobrée, *Modern Prose Style*], *Spec*, No. 5546 (Oct. 12), p. 536.

C495 "New Novels" [R.], *Listener*, XII (Oct. 17), 670.

C496 "New Stories" [R., incl. William Faulkner, *Dr. Martino*; Isak Dinesen, *Seven Gothic Tales*], *Listener*, XII (Oct. 31), 756.

C497 "Oswald Spengler" [E.], *European Qtly*, I (Nov.), 143-52.

C498 "The Present Language of Poetry" [E.], *Lond Mer*, XXXI (Nov.), 34-39.

C499 "The Problem of Scotland" [R., George Blake, *The Heart of Scotland*; and William Power, *Scotland and the Scots*], *Spec*, No. 5549 (Nov. 2), p. 676.

C500 "New Novels" [R., incl. Robert Graves, *Claudius the God*], *Listener*, XII (Nov. 14), 840.

C501 [Obituary letter on A. R. Orage], *New English Weekly*, VI (Nov. 15), 119.

C502 "Double Vision" [P.], *Lond Mer*, XXXI (Dec.), 114-15.
Reprinted in *The Year's Poetry*, ed. D. K. Roberts, *et al*. London, 1935.

C503 "New Novels" [R.], *Listener*, XII (Dec. 5), 966.

C504 "New Novels" [R., incl. Thornton Wilder, *Heaven's My Destination*], *Listener*, XII (Dec. 19), 1050.

C505 "The Victorian Novel" [R., Lord David Cecil, *Early Victorian Novelists*], *Spec*, No. 5557 (Dec. 28), p. 1000.

1935

C506 "The Harvest" [P.], *Mod Scot*, V (Jan.), 266-67.
Reprinted in *The Year's Poetry*, ed. D. K. Roberts, *et al*. London, 1935.

C507 "New Novels" [R., incl. D. H. Lawrence, *A Modern Lover*; and Fr. Rolfe, *The Desire and Pursuit of the Whole*], *Listener*, XIII (Jan. 2), 44.

C508 "A New Way with Poetry: The Confusion of Modern Criticism" [E.], *Scots*, Jan. 3, p. 11.

C509 "New Novels" [R.], *Listener*, XIII (Jan. 16), 128.

C510 "New Novels" [R.], *Listener*, XIII (Jan. 30), 211.

C511 "Ernst Toller" [R., Ernst Toller, *Seven Plays*], *Scots*, Jan. 31, p. 13.

C512 "Hölderlin's *Patmos*" [E.], *European Qtly*, I (Feb.), 241-55.

C513 "Society and the Poet" [R., Stephen Spender, *Vienna*; Edith Sitwell, *Aspects of Modern Poetry*], *Lond Mer*, XXXI (Feb.), 382-84.

C514 "Scotland's Winter" [P.], *Listener*, XIII (Feb. 6), 226.
Reprinted in *Poems of Tomorrow*, ed. Janet Adam Smith. London, 1935.

C515 "New Novels" [R.], *Listener*, XIII (Feb. 13), 300.

C516 "D. H. Lawrence: A Portrait by his Wife" [R., Frieda Lawrence, *Not I, But the Wind*], *Scots*, Feb. 14, p. 13.

C517 "New Novels" [R.], *Listener*, XIII (Feb. 27), 384.

C518 "An Essayist of Our Time" [R., Desmond MacCarthy, *Experience*], *Lond Mer*, XXXI (March), 476-77.

C519 "Lewis Grassic Gibbon. An Appreciation," *Scottish Standard*, I (March), 23-24.

C520 "Odious Comparisons" [R., R. D. Jameson, *Comparisons of Literature*], *Scots*, March 7, p. 15.

C521 "New Novels" [R., incl. Christopher Isherwood, *Mr. Norris Changes Trains*], *Listener*, XIII (March 13), 468.

C522 "The Brighton Fable" [R., Osbert Sitwell and Margaret Barton, *Brighton*], *Scots*, March 21, p. 8.

C523 "C. Day Lewis" [R., C. Day Lewis, *Collected Poems* and *A Time To Dance*], *Spec*, No. 5569 (March 22), pp. 496, 498.

C524 "New Novels" [R., incl. Thomas Mann, *The Young Joseph*; and Eric Linklater, *Ripeness Is All*], *Listener*, XIII (March 27), 552.

C525 "Experimental Poetry" [R., Herbert Read, *Poems, 1914-1934*; and Ezra Pound, *A Draft of Cantos, XXXI-XLI*], *Lond Mer*, XXXI (April), 594-95.

C526 "Pages from a Scottish Journey (I, Glasgow; II, Scottish Nationalism)," *Mod Scot*, VI (April), 18-28.

C527 "News About Authors" [R., Frank Swinnerton, *The Georgian Literary Scene*], *Scots*, April 1, p. 13.

C528 "New Novels" [R.], *Listener*, XIII (April 10), 636.

C529 "Regency Architecture" [R.], *Scots*, April 11, p. 13.

C530 "New Novels" [R., incl. William Faulkner, *Pylon*], *Listener*, XIII (April 24), 720.

C531 "Henry James as Critic" [R., Henry James, *Critical Prefaces*], *Scots*, April 29, p. 13.

C532 "Literature from 1910 to 1935" [E.], *Scots*, May 4 (Silver Jubilee Supplement), p. xiii.

C533 "New Novels" [R.], *Listener*, XIII (May 8), 814.

C534 "Sir Walter Raleigh" [R.], *Scots*, May 9, p. 13.

C535 "The Destructive Element" [R., Stephen Spender, *The Destructive Element*], *Spec*, No. 5576 (May 10), p. 796.

C536 "New Novels" [R.], *Listener*, XIII (May 22), 898.

C537 "Childhood's World" [R., Walter de la Mare, *Early One Morning*], *Scots*, May 23, p. 15.
Cf. C540.

C538 "Fletcher of Saltoun" [R.], *Spec*, No. 5579 (May 31), p. 949.

C539 "Poetry of George Barker" [R., George Barker, *Poems*], *Lond Mer*, XXXII (June), 187.

C540 "Childhood" [R., Walter de la Mare, *Early One Morning*], *Lond Mer*, XXXII (June), 174-75.
Cf. C537.

C541 "New Novels" [R.], *Listener*, XIII (June 5), 986.

C542 "Sir Thomas More" [R., R. W. Chambers, *Sir Thomas More*], *Scots*, June 6, p. 13.

C543 "The Hill" [P.], *Spec*, No. 5580 (June 7), p. 980.

C544 "New Short Stories" [R.], *Listener*, XIII (June 19), 1070.

C545 "Arnold Bennett" [R., D. C. Bennett, *Arnold Bennett*], *Scots*, June 24, p. 15.

C546 "Murder in the Cathedral" [R., T. S. Eliot, *Murder in the Cathedral*], *Lond Mer*, XXXII (July), 281-83.

C547 "The Earl of Rochester" [R., Vivian de Sola Pinto, *Rochester*], *Scots*, July 8, p. 15.

C548 "New Novels" [R., incl. Graham Greene, *England Made Me*], *Listener*, XIV (July 10), 88.

C549 "The Journey" [P.], *Spec*, No. 5586 (July 19), p. 93.

C550 "American Literature" [R., F. L. Pattee, *First Century of American Literature*], *Scots*, July 22, p. 15.
Cf. C161.

C551 "New Novels" [R., incl. I. Compton-Burnett, *A House and Its Head*], *Listener*, XIV (July 24), 174.

C552 "Views and Reviews" [E.], *New English Weekly*, VII (July 25), 291-92.

C553 "War in the Desert" [R., T. E. Lawrence, *Seven Pillars of Wisdom*], *Scots*, July 29, p. 8.

C554 "New Novels" [R., incl. Henri de Montherlant, *Lament for the Death of an Upper Class*], *Listener*, XIV (Aug. 7), 254.

C555 "What Is Poetry?" [R., *The Poet's Tongue*, ed. W. H. Auden and John Garrett], *Scots*, Aug. 15, p. 11.

C556 "New Novels" [R.], *Listener*, XIV (Aug. 21), 334.

C557 "Time Song" [P.], *Listener*, XIV (Aug. 28), 339.

C558 "I and Not I" [P.], *Lond Mer*, XXXII (Sept.), 421-22.

C559 "New Novels" [R., incl. Thomas Wolfe, *Of Time and the River*], *Listener*, XIV (Sept. 4), 416.

C560 "The Lamb Letters" [R., *The Letters of Charles Lamb*, ed. E. V. Lucas], *Scots*, Sept. 12, p. 13.

C561 "New Novels" [R.], *Listener*, XIV (Sept. 18), 500.

C562 "Views and Reviews" [E. on Goethe's *Faust*], *New English Weekly*, VII (Sept. 26), 391-92.

C563 "Mr. Sitwell's Tirades [R., Osbert Sitwell, *Penny Foolish*], *Scots*, Sept. 26, p. 13.

C564 "Merlin" [P.], *Spec*, No. 5596 (Sept. 27), p. 461. Reprinted in *The Year's Poetry*, ed., D. K. Roberts *et al*. London, 1936.

C565 "New Novels" [R.], *Listener*, XIV (Oct. 2), 583.

C566 "Shakespeare's Imagery" [R., Caroline Spurgeon, *Shakespeare's Imagery*], *Scots*, Oct. 7, p. 13.

C567 "New Novels" [R., incl. William Faulkner, *As I Lay Dying*; and David Garnett, *Beany-Eye*], *Listener*, XIV (Oct. 16), 681.

C568 "Genealogy of the Fool" [R.], *Scots*, Oct. 17, p. 6.

C569 "New Novels" [R.], *Listener*, XIV (Oct. 30), 777.

C570 "Views and Reviews" [E. on Dostoyevsky], *New English Weekly*, VIII (Oct. 31), 50-51.

C571 "A Romantic Poet" [R., Peter Quennell, *Byron: The Years of Fame*], *Scots*, Oct. 31, p. 15.

C572 "Criticism and Criticism" [R., F. O. Matthiessen, *The Achievement of T. S. Eliot*; Geoffrey Grigson, *The Arts Today*], *Lond Mer*, XXXIII (Nov.), 74-76.
Cf. C996.

C573 "Glasgow Slums" [R., Alexander McArthur and H. Kingsley Long, *No Mean City*], *Spec*, No. 5602 (Nov. 8), p. 788.
An unsigned review, identified from the *Spectator* MSS book.

C574 "New Novels" [R., incl. Herbert Read, *The Green Child*], *Listener*, XIV (Nov. 13), 889.

C575 "Recent Poetry" [R.], *Scots*, Nov. 21, p. 13.

C576 "New Novels" [R.], *Listener*, XIV (Nov. 27), 985.

C577 "Thomas Gray" [R., *The Correspondence of Thomas Gray*, ed. Paget Toynbee and Leonard Whibley], *Lond Mer*, XXXIII (Dec.), 206-07.

C578 "A Neglected Genius" [R., *The Works of T. L. Beddoes*, ed. H. W. Donner; H. W. Donner, *T. L. Beddoes*], *Scots*, Dec. 5, p. 6.

C579 "New Novels" [R.], *Listener*, XIV (Dec. 11), 1081.

C580 "Keats' Letters" [R.], *Scots*, Dec. 30, p. 11.

1936

C581 [R., G. M. Thomson, *Scotland: That Distressed Area*], *Criterion*, XV (Jan.), 330-32.

C582 "New Short Stories" [R.], *Listener*, XV (Jan. 1), 44.

C583 "Modernism" [R., Janko Lavrin, *Aspects of Modernism*], *Scots*, Jan. 9, p. 13.

C584 "New Novels" [R.], *Listener*, XV (Jan. 15), 140.

C585 "John Freeman" [R.], *Scots*, Jan. 23, p. 13.

C586 "New Novels" [R.], *Listener*, XV (Jan. 30), 230.

C587 "Epilogue" [R., *Epilogue*, ed. Laura Riding and Robert Graves], *Lond Mer*, XXXIII (Feb.), 451.
     Cf. C626.

C588 "Rudyard Kipling" [E.], *Listener*, XV (Feb. 5), 272.

C589 "New Novels" [R.], *Listener*, XV (Feb. 12), 324.

C590 "Shakespeare" [R., J. Middleton Murry, *Shakespeare*], *Scots*, Feb. 13, p. 13.
     Cf. C594.

C591 "A Literary Observer" [R.], *Scots*, Feb. 24, p. 13.

C592 "New Novels" [R.], *Listener*, XV (Feb. 26), 416.

C593 "Four Poems" ["I. This conqueror holding me from head to toe. II. O you my law. III. See, all the silver roads wind in. IV. No more of this trapped gazing"], *Lond Mer*, XXXIII (March), 477-79.

C594 "Shakespeare" [R., J. Middleton Murry, *Shakespeare*], *Lond Mer*, XXXIII (March), 540-41.
     Cf. C590.

C595 "New Novels" [R.], *Listener*, XV (March 11), 512.

C596 "Mr. H. W. Nevinson" [R.], *Scots*, March 12, p. 13.

C597 "The Flood" [R., C. Day Lewis, *Noah and the Waters*], *Spec*, No. 5620 (March 13), p. 482, 484.

C598 "New Novels" [R.], *Listener*, XV (March 25), 604.

C599 "An Urbane Realist" [R., E. M. Forster, *Abinger Harvest*], *Scots*, March 26, p. 6.

C600 "Two Anthologies" [R., *The Faber Book of Modern Verse*, ed. Michael Roberts; *A Treasury of Modern Poetry*, ed. R. L. Mégroz], *Lond Mer*, XXXIII (April), 638-39.

C601 "Mr. Herbert Read on Shelley" [R., Herbert Read, *In Defence of Shelley*], *Outlook*, I (April), 83-86.

C602 "Mr. Eliot's Poetry" [R., T. S. Eliot, *Collected Poems*], *Spec*, No. 5623 (April 3), p. 622.

C603 "New Novels" [R.], *Listener*, XV (April 8), 696.

C604 "Columbus" [R.], *Scots*, April 9, p. 15.

C605 "De Quincey's Genius" [R., Edward Sackville West, *A Flame in Sunlight*], *Scots*, April 27, p. 13.

C606 "New Novels" [R.], *Listener*, XV (April 29), 843.

C607 "New Novels" [R.], *Listener*, XV (May 13), 938.

C608 "Translation of Poetry" [R., Charles Baudelaire, *Flowers of Evil*, trans. George Dillon and Edna St. Vincent Millay], *Scots*, May 14, p. 15.

C609 "The Journey" [P.], *Spec*, No. 5629 (May 15), p. 886.

C610 "New Novels" [R.], *Listener*, XV (May 27), 1032.

C611 "A High Monologue" [R., W. B. Yeats, *Autobiographical Papers*], *Scots*, May 28, p. 15.

C612 "Mr. Michael Roberts' *Poems*" [R.], *Lond Mer*, XXXIV (June), 168.

C613 "A Literature Without a Language" [E.], *Outlook*, I (June), 84-89.
      Correspondence, (July), 92-94; (Oct.), 55; and Muir's reply, (Aug.), 68-70.

C614 "New Novels" [R.], *Listener*, XV (June 10), 1130.

C615 "New Novels" [R.], *Listener*, XV (June 24), 1223.

C616 "Joan of Arc" [R., Victoria Sackville West, *St. Joan of Arc*], *Scots*, June 11, p. 15.

C617 "Five Poets" [R.], *Scots*, July 2, p. 15.

C618 "Poem" ["O! I have seen the heaven of good deeds spread"], *Outlook*, I (July), 98-99.

C619 "New Novels" [R., incl. Aldous Huxley, *Eyeless in Gaza*], *Listener*, XVI (July 8), 92.

C620 "Lawrence of Arabia" [R., Vyvyan Richards, *Portrait of T. E. Lawrence*], *Scots*, July 9, p. 13.

C621 "New Novels" [R., incl. Hugo von Hofmannsthal, *Andreas*], *Listener*, XVI (July 22), 186.

C622 "Sir William Watson" [R., Sir William Watson, *Poems*], *Scots*, July 27, p. 13.

C623 "First Poems of Mr. Prokosch" [R., Frederick Prokosch, *The Assassins*], *Lond Mer*, XXXIV (Aug.), 365.

C624 "New Novels" [R., incl. Graham Greene, *A Gun for Sale*], *Listener*, XVI (Aug. 5), 278.

C625 "New Novels" [R.], *Listener*, XVI (Aug. 19), 364.

C626 "Epilogue" [R., *Epilogue* (Vol. II), ed. Laura Riding], *Outlook*, I (Sept.), 87-89.
      Cf. C587.

C627 "New Novels" [R.], *Listener*, XVI (Sept. 9), 500.

C628 "Fruits of Reading" [R.], *Scots*, Sept. 14, p. 13.

C629 "This Changing Stage" [R., Allardyce Nicoll, *The English Stage*], *Scots*, Sept. 28, p. 13.

C630 "New Novels" [R.], *Listener*, XVI (Sept. 16), 547.

C631 "New Novels" [R.], *Listener*, XVI (Sept. 30), 644.

C632 "The Town Betrayed" [P.], *Lond Mer*, XXXIV (Oct.), 486-87.

C633 "Orage" [R., Philip Mairet, *A. R. Orage*], *Outlook*, I (Oct.), 95-97.

C634 "George Moore" [R., Joseph Hone, *George Moore*], *Scots*, Oct. 5, p. 13.

C635 "From Donne to Keats" [R., F. R. Leavis, *Revaluation*], *Scots*, Oct. 15, p. 15.

C636 "New Novels" [R.], *Listener*, XVI (Oct. 21), 786.

C637 "New Novels" [R., incl. Djuna Barnes, *Nightwood*; and Robert Graves, *Antigua, Penny, Puce*], *Listener*, XVI (Oct. 28), 832.

C638 "A French Poet's World" [R., Stéphane Mallarmé, *Poems*, trans. Roger Fry], *Scots*, Oct. 29, p. 15.

C639 "Burns and Holy Willie" [E.], *Left Review*, II (Nov.), 762-64.

C640 "A. E. Housman" [R., A. E. Housman, *More Poems*; and A. S. F. Gow, *A. E. Housman*], *Lond Mer*, XXXV (Nov.), 62-63.

C641 "The Problems of Criticism" [R., David Daiches, *New Literary Values*], *Outlook*, I (Nov.), 70-72.

C642 "G. K. C." [R., *The Autobiography of G. K. Chesterton*], *Scots*, Nov. 5, p. 15.

C643 "Three American Novels" [R., incl. John Dos Passos, *The Big Money*], *Listener*, XVI (Nov. 18), 970.

C644 "Rilke Translated" [R., Rainer Maria Rilke, *Sonnets to Orpheus*, trans. J. B. Leishman], *Scots*, Nov. 23, p. 15.

C645 "New Novels" [R.], *Listener*, XVI (Nov. 25), 1018.

C646 "Mr. Sitwell's Poems" [R., Sacheverell Sitwell, *Collected Poems*], *Lond Mer*, XXXV (Dec.), 200-01.

C647 "Mr. Auden's Poems" [R., W. H. Auden, *Look, Stranger!*], *Spec*, No. 5658 (Dec. 4), p. 1008.

C648 "New Novels" [R.], *Listener*, XVI (Dec. 16), 1162.

C649 "The Tree of Peace" [R., Aldous Huxley, *The Olive Tree*], *Scots*, Dec. 17, p. 15.

C650 "New Verse" [R., William Plomer, *Visiting the Caves*; Lilian Bowes Lyon, *Bright Feather Fading*; Richard Eberhart, *Reading the Spirit*], *Spec*, No. 5661 (Dec. 25), pp. 1131-32.

C651 "Scott's Critics" [R., J. T. Hillhouse, *The Waverley Novels and Their Critics*], *Scots*, Dec. 31, p. 11.

1937

C652 "Hölderlin's Journey" [P.], *Criterion*, XVI (Jan.), 267-68.
Reprinted in *The Year's Poetry*, ed. D. K. Roberts, *et al.* London, 1937.

C653 "Poem" ["O! I have seen the heaven of good deeds spread"], *Poetry* (Chicago), XLIX (Jan.), 196-98.

C654 "New Novels" [R.], *Listener*, XVII (Jan. 6), 44.

C655 "Ibsen" [P.], *Listener*, XVII (Jan. 13), 62.

C656 "Fanny Brawne" [R.], *Scots*, Jan. 14, p. 13.

C657 "New Novels" [R.], *Listener*, XVII (Jan. 20), 140.

C658 "New Novels" [R.], *Listener*, XVII (Feb. 3), 240.

C659 "Gerard Manley Hopkins" [R., *The Notebooks and Papers of Gerard Manley Hopkins*, ed. Humphry House], *Scots*, Feb. 4, p. 15.
Cf. C663.

C660 "New Novels" [R.], *Listener*, XVII (Feb. 17), 334.

C661 "Poetry and Religion" [R.], *Scots*, Feb. 18, p. 15.

C662 "Troy" [P.], *Lond Mer*, XXXV (March), 450-51.

C663 "Hopkins's Notebooks" [R.], *Lond Mer*, XXXV (March), 511-2.
Cf. C659.

C664 "New Novels" [R.], *Listener*, XVII (March 10), 482.

C665 "Life and Letters" [R., Ezra Pound, *Polite Essays*], *Scots*, March 11, p. 17.

C666 "Mary Stuart" [P.], *Spec*, No. 5672 (March 12), p. 469.

C667 "Russian Writers" [R.], *Scots*, March 18, p. 15.

C668 "Poem" ["It might be the day after the last day"], *Spec*, No. 5673 (March 19), p. 514.

C669 "New Novels" [R., incl. Eric Linklater, *Juan in China*], *Listener*, XVII (March 24), 576.

C670 "New Novels" [R., incl. Virginia Woolf, *The Years*; and I. Compton-Burnett, *Daughters and Sons*], *Listener*, XVII (March 31), 622.

C671 "An American Poet" [R., Edgar Lee Masters, *Whitman*], *Scots*, April 1, p. 15.

C672 "New Novels" [R.], *Listener*, XVII (April 14), 725.

C673 "New Novels" [R.], *Listener*, XVII (April 28), 832.

C674 "Aspects of Life" [R.], *Scots*, April 29, p. 17.

C675 "Prophetic Poetry" [R., H. J. C. Grierson, *Milton and Words-worth*], *Lond Mer*, XXXVI (May), 83-84.

C676 "New Novels" [R.], *Listener*, XVII (May 12), 944.

C677 "Jonathan Swift" [R., Bertram Newman, *Jonathan Swift*], *Scots*, May 13, p. 13.

C678 "New Novels" [R.], *Listener*, XVII (May 26), 1055.

C679 "Troy" [P.], *Listener*, XVII (June 2), 1103.

C680 "G. K. Chesterton" [R., Émile Cammaerts, *The Laughing Prophet*], *Scots*, June 3, p. 15.

C681 "New Novels" [R.], *Listener*, XVII (June 9), 1164.

C682 "Challenge to Islam" [R.], *Scots*, June 17, p. 15.

C683 "The Late Sir James Barrie" [Full-page obituary], *Scots*, June 21, p. 7.
        Unsigned; identified by the *Scotsman* for the present bibliography.

C684 "New Novels" [R.], *Listener*, XVII (June 23), 1276.

C685 "Mr. Madge's Poems" [R., Charles Madge, *The Disappearing Castle*], *Lond Mer*, XXXVI (July), 294-95.

C686 "New Novels" [R.], *Listener*, XVIII (July 7), 47.

C687 "Daniel Defoe" [R., James R. Sutherland, *Daniel Defoe*], *Scots*, July 8, p. 15.

C688 "New Novels" [R.], *Listener*, XVIII (July 21), 157.

C689 "Two Poets" [R., R. P. Eckerts, *Edward Thomas*; and *Collected Works of Isaac Rosenberg*], *Scots*, July 22, p. 15.

C690 "Culture and Capitalism" [R., *The Mind in Chains*, ed. C. Day Lewis], *Spec*, No. 5692 (July 30), p. 211.

C691 "New Novels" [R.], *Listener*, XVIII (Aug. 4), 263.

C692 "New Novels" [R.], *Listener*, XVIII (Aug. 18), 367.

C693 "English Painting" [R.], *Scots*, Aug. 19, p. 13.

C694 "New Novels" [R.], *Listener*, XVIII (Sept. 1), 471.

C695 "Shakespeare's Problems" [R., Kenneth Muir and Sean O'Loughlin, *The Voyage to Illyria*], *Scots*, Sept. 2, p. 13.

C696 "New Novels" [R.], *Listener*, XVIII (Sept. 22), 637.

C697 "New Novels" [R.], *Listener*, XVIII (Sept. 29), 693.

C698 "Marlowe's Spirit" [R.], *Scots*, Sept. 30, p. 15.

C699 [R., incl. Ezra Pound, *Fifth Decad of Cantos*; Louis MacNeice, *Out of the Picture*; Rex Warner, *Poems*; W. H. Auden, *Spain*; Federico Garcia Lorca, *Lament for the Death of a Bullfighter*, trans. A. L. Lloyd], *Criterion*, XVII (Oct.), 148-54.

C700 "New Novels" [R.], *Listener*, XVIII (Oct. 13), 807.

C701 "Mr. Yeats's Vision" [R., W. B. Yeats, *A Vision*], *Scots*, Oct. 18, p. 13.

C702 "New Novels" [R., incl. Ernest Hemingway, *To Have and Have Not*], *Listener*, XVIII (Oct. 27), 925.

C703 "Letters. I and II" [P.], *Lond Mer*, XXXVII (Nov.), 6-7.

C704 [Comment on W. H. Auden], *New Verse*, Nos. 26-27 ["Auden Double Number"] (Nov.), p. 23.

C705 "Æ" [R., Æ, *Living Torch*; John Eglinton, *Memoir of Æ*], *Scots*, Nov. 1, p. 13.

C706 "Fashions in Reading" [E.], *Scots*, Nov. 5, p. 7.

C707 "New Short Stories" [R., incl. Christopher Isherwood, *Sally Bowles*], *Listener*, XVIII (Nov. 10), 1039.

C708 "New Novels" [R.], *Listener*, XVIII (Nov. 24), 1157.

C709 "Knox in Scottish History" [R., Lord Eustace Percy, *John Knox*], *Lond Mer*, XXXVII (Dec.), 213-14.

C710 "Gorgeous Days" [R.], *Scots*, Dec. 2, p. 15.

C711 "New Novels" [R.], *Listener*, XVIII (Dec. 8), 1275.

C712 "Drama and Theatre" [R.], *Scots*, Dec. 16, p. 15.

C713 "New Novels" [R., incl. Henri de Montherlant, *Pity for Women*], *Listener*, XVIII (Dec. 22), 1394.

C714 "Scottish Literature" [R., Friederich Brie, *Die Nationale Literatur Schottlands*], *Scots*, Dec. 27, p. 13.

1938

C715 "Conrad" [R., *Conrad's Prefaces*, ed. Richard Garnett], *Lond Mer*, XXXVII (Jan.), 354.

C716 "Poem" ["If a good man were ever housed in Hell"], *New Verse*, No. 28 (Jan.), p. 3.

C717 "Short Stories" [R.], *Listener*, XIX (Jan. 5), 47.

C718 "New Novels" [R.], *Listener*, XIX (Jan. 19), 159.

C719 "Post-War Pessimism" [E.], *Listener*, XIX (Jan. 26), 185-86.

C720 "Self-Portrait" [R., W. S. Maugham, *The Summing Up*], *Scots*, Jan. 27, p. 15.

C721 "New Novels" [R.], *Listener*, XIX (Feb. 2), 267.

C722 "The Paragon" [R.], *Scots*, Feb. 10, p. 15.

C723 "New Novels" [R.], *Listener*, XIX (Feb. 16), 381.

C724 "New Novels" [R.], *Listener*, XIX (March 9), 539.

C725 "Shakespeare's Art in the Comedies" [R., H. B. Charlton, *Shakespearian Comedy*], *Scots*, March 10, p. 17.

C726 "New Novels" [R., incl. Samuel Beckett, *Murphy*], *Listener*, XIX (March 16), 597.

C727 "Education of a Novelist" [R., Christopher Isherwood, *Lions and Shadows*], *Listener*, Spring Book Supplement (March 16), vii.

C728 "Poem" ["Day after day we kept the dusty road"], *Spec*, No. 5726 (March 25), p. 511.

C729 "Rainer Maria Rilke" [R., William Rose and G. Craig Houston, *Rainer Maria Rilke*], *Scots*, March 28, p. 15.
Cf. C731.

C730 "New Novels" [R.], *Listener*, XIX (March 30), 707.

C731 "Rilke" [R., Rose and Houston, *Rainer Maria Rilke*], *Lond Mer*, XXXVII (April), 649-50.
Cf. C729.

C732 "New Novels" [R., incl. Robert Graves, *Count Belisarius*], *Listener*, XIX (April 13), 819.

C733 "Two Poets" [R.], *Scots*, April 25, p. 15.

C734 "New Novels" [R.], *Listener*, XIX (April 27), 927.

C735 "The Court Favourite" [Broadcast talk on Queen Victoria's John Brown], *Listener*, XIX (May 4), 945.

C736 "Gerard Manley Hopkins" [R., G. M. Hopkins, *Further Letters*, ed. C. C. Abbott], *Scots*, May 9, p. 15.

C737 "New Novels" [R.], *Listener*, XIX (May 11), 1034.

C738 "Values in Humanism" [R., J. W. Mackail, *Studies in Humanism*], *Scots*, May 23, p. 15.

C739 "New Novels" [R.], *Listener*, XIX (May 25), 1146.

C740 "Poem" ["Early in spring the little General came"], *Listener*, XIX (June 9), 1232.

C741 "German Poetry" [R., incl. David Gascoyne, *Hölderlin's Madness*; *Rilke's Poems*, trans. J. B. Leishman], *Scots*, June 13, p. 15.

C742 "New Novels" [R.], *Listener*, XIX (June 16), 1304.

C743 "T. E. Hulme" [R., Michael Roberts, *T. E. Hulme*], *Scots*, June 23, p. 15.

C744 "The Scottish Character" [E.], *Listener*, XIX (June 23), 1323-25.

C745 "New Novels" [R.], *Listener*, XIX (June 30), 1413.

C746 "Mr. Gogarty's Poems" [R.], *Lond Mer*, XXXVIII (July), 265-66.

C747 "Hölderlin" [E.], *New Verse*, No. 30 (Summer), pp. 13-16.

C748 "Thomas Hardy" [R., W. R. Rutland, *Thomas Hardy*], *Scots*, July 4, p. 15.

C749 "New Novels" [R.], *Listener*, XX (July 7), 45.

C750 "New Novels" [R., incl. Richard Hughes, *In Hazard*; and Graham Greene, *Brighton Rock*], *Listener*, XX (July 21), 153.

C751 "D. H. Lawrence" [R., Knud Merrild, *A Poet and Two Painters*], *Scots*, July 28, p. 15.

C752 "New Novels" [R.], *Listener*, XX (Aug. 4), 252.

C753 "New Novels" [R.], *Listener*, XX (Aug. 18), 357.

C754 "New Novels" [R., incl. Daphne DuMaurier, *Rebecca*], *Listener*, XX (Sept. 1), 461.

C755 "Function of Poetry" [R., John Crowe Ransom, *The World's Body*], *Scots*, Sept. 1, p. 13.

C756 "New Novels" [R., incl. T. H. White, *The Sword in the Stone*], *Listener*, XX (Sept. 15), 571.

C757 "Criticism and Prophecy" [R., J. Middleton Murry, *Heaven—And Earth*], *Scots*, Sept. 15, p. 13.

C758 "New Novels" [R.], *Listener*, XX (Sept. 29), 678.

C759 "La Vie de Boheme" [R., Robert McAlmon, *Being Geniuses Together*], *Scots*, Oct. 6, p. 15.

C760 "New Novels" [R.], *Listener*, XX (Oct. 13), 795.

C761 "The Part of Death" [R., C. Day Lewis, *Overture to Death*], *Listener*, Early Autumn Book Supplement (Oct. 13), p. xii.

C762 "New Novels" [R.], *Listener*, XX (Oct. 27), 913.

C763 "New Novels" [R.], *Listener*, XX (Nov. 10), 1027.

C764 "T. E. Lawrence" [R., *Letters of T. E. Lawrence*, ed. David Garnett], *Scots*, Nov. 21, p. 13.

C765 "A Lyrical Critic" [R., J. Cowper Powys, *The Pleasures of Literature*], *Scots*, Nov. 28, p. 13.

C766 "Mr. Graves's Poems" [R., Robert Graves, *Collected Poems*], *Lond Mer*, XXXIX (Dec.), 215-16.

C767 "New Short Stories" [R.], *Listener*, XX (Dec. 1), 1201.

C768 "Friedrich Hölderlin" [R., Ronald Peacock, *Hölderlin*], *Scots*, Dec. 5, p. 13.

C769 "New Novels" [R.], *Listener*, XX (Dec. 8), 1262.

C770 "New Novels" [R.], *Listener*, XX (Dec. 22), 1377.

1939

C771 "Chateaubriand" [R., André Maurois, *Chateaubriand*], *Scots*, Jan. 2, p. 13.

C772 "New Novels" [R.], *Listener*, XXI (Jan. 5), 45.

C773 "New Novels" [R.], *Listener*, XXI (Jan. 19), 169.

C774 "A Modern Poet on Modern Poetry" [R., Louis MacNeice, *Modern Poetry*], *Lond Mer*, XXXIX (Feb.), 449-50.

C775 "Shakespeare" [R.], *Scots*, Feb. 2, p. 15.

C776 "New Novels" [R.], *Listener*, XXI (Feb. 9), 329.

C777 "New Novels" [R.], *Listener*, XXI (Feb. 16), 385.

C778 "New Novels" [R., incl. I. Compton-Burnett, *A Family and A Fortune*], *Listener*, XXI (March 2), 489.

C779 "Will Davenant" [R.], *Scots*, March 2, p. 15.

C780 "New Novels" [R., incl. Allen Tate, *The Fathers*; and Christopher Isherwood, *Goodbye to Berlin*], *Listener*, XXI (March 16), 597.

C781 "Duty and the Writer" [R., Storm Jameson, *Civil Journey*], *Listener*, Spring Book Supplement (March 16), p. xv.

C782 "Genius of Stendhal" [R.], *Scots*, March 16, p. 15.

C783 "Mr. Eliot's New Play" [R., T. S. Eliot, *The Family Reunion*], *Scots*, March 23, p. 6.

C784 "New Novels" [R., incl. William Faulkner, *The Wild Palms*], *Listener*, XXI (March 30), 701.

C785 "The Narrow Country" [P.], *Lond Mer*, XXXIX (April), 583.

C786 "New Novels" [R.], *Listener*, XXI (April 13), 805.

C787 "New Novels" [R.], *Listener*, XXI (April 27), 909.

C788 "Lessing as Critic" [R., J. G. Robertson, *Lessing's Dramatic Theory*], *Scots*, April 27, p. 15.

C789 "The Burden" [P.], *Listener*, XXI (May 4), 938.

C790 "James Joyce's New Novel" [R., James Joyce, *Finnegan's Wake*], *Listener*, XXI (May 11), 1013.

C791 "The Nature of Poetry" [R., Jacob Bronowski, *The Poet's Defence*], *Scots*, May 22, p. 15.

C792 "New Novels" [R.], *Listener*, XXI (May 25), 1125.

C793 "New Novels" [R., incl. Katherine Anne Porter, *Pale Horse, Pale Rider*], *Listener*, XXI (June 8), 1233.

C794 "Rainer Maria Rilke" [R., Rainer Maria Rilke, *Duino Elegies*, trans. J. B. Leishman and Stephen Spender], *Scots*, June 12, p. 15.

C795 "New Novels" [R.], *Listener*, XXI (June 22), 1337.

C796 "New Novels" [R., incl. Ernest Hemingway, *The Fifth Column*], *Listener*, XXII (July 6), 45.

C797 "The Old Wordsworth" [R.], *Scots*, July 6, p. 13.

C798   "New Novels" [R.], *Listener*, XXII (July 20), 149.

C799   "New Novels" [R.], *Listener*, XXII (Aug. 3), 249.

C800   "Jane Austen's Art" [R., Mary Lascelles, *Jane Austen*], *Scots*, Aug. 10, p. 13.

C801   "New Novels" [R., incl. Joyce Cary, *Mister Johnson*], *Listener*, XXII (Aug. 17), 345.

C802   "Poetry and Life" [R., G. Wilson Knight, *The Burning Oracle*], *Scots*, Aug. 24, p. 13.

C803   "New Novels" [R.], *Listener*, XXII (Sept. 7), 493.

C804   "The Nature of Comedy" [R.], *Scots*, Sept. 7, p. 9.

C805   "New Novels" [R., incl. John Steinbeck, *The Grapes of Wrath*], *Listener*, XXII (Sept. 14), 543.

C806   "New Novels" [R.], *Listener*, XXII (Sept. 28), 638.

C807   "The Refugees" [P.], *New Alliance*, I (Autumn), 61-65.
Consists of "Chorus" (45 ll.), "The Mother" (20 ll.), "The Father" (15 ll.), "1st Voice" (2 ll.), "2nd Voice" (6 ll.), "3rd Voice" (17 ll.), "Chorus."
Only the last "Chorus" has been reprinted.

C808   "New Novels" [R.], *Listener*, XXII (Oct. 12), 734.

C809   "New Novels" [R., incl. Aldous Huxley, *After Many a Summer*], *Listener*, XXII (Oct. 26), 833.

C810   "New Novels" [R.], *Listener*, XXII (Nov. 9), 934.

C811   "German Writers" [R., Jethro Bithell, *Modern German Literature*], *Scots*, Nov. 20, p. 7.

C812   "New Novels" [R.], *Listener*, XXII (Nov. 23), 1038.

C813   "New Novels" [R.], *Listener*, XXII (Dec. 7), 1140.

C814   "New Novels" [R.], *Listener*, XXII (Dec. 21), 1242.

1940

C815   "New Novels" [R.], *Listener*, XXIII (Jan. 11), 90.

C816   "New Novels" [R., incl. Hugh Kingsmill, *The Fall*], *Listener*, XXIII (Jan. 25), 190.

C817   "New Novels" [R.], *Listener*, XXIII (Feb. 8), 286.

C818   "New Novels" [R.], *Listener*, XXIII (Feb. 22), 388.

C819   "Then" [P.], *New Alliance*, I (March), 8.

C820   "New Novels" [R., incl. Graham Greene, *The Power and the Glory*], *Listener*, XXIII (March 7), 490.

C821   "New Novels" [R.], *Listener*, XXIII (March 21), 597.

C822 "Time and the Modern Novel" [E.], *Atlantic Monthly*, CLXV
(April), 535-37.
A revision of C484.
C823 "New Novels" [R.], *Listener*, XXIII (April 11), 754.
C824 "New Novels" [R.], *Listener*, XXIII (April 18), 806.
C825 "New Novels" [R.], *Listener*, XXIII (May 9), 946.
C826 "Short Stories" [R.], *Listener*, XXIII (May 16), 986.
C827 "New Novels" [R.], *Listener*, XXIII (May 23), 1027.
C828 "Poems. I. Robert the Bruce Stricken with Leprosy: To Douglas.
II. Rimbaud," *New Alliance*, I (June-July), 9.
C829 "New Novels" [R.], *Listener*, XXIII (June 6), 1103.
C830 "The Eternal Recurrence" [P.], *Listener*, XXIII (June 13), 1130.
C831 "New Novels" [R.], *Listener*, XXIII (June 27), 1211.
C832 "New Novels" [R.], *Listener*, XXIV (July 11), 67.
C833 "Animals and Magic" [R., Forrest Reid, *Private Road*], *Spec*, No.
5847 (July 19), p. 68.
C834 "New Novels" [R.], *Listener*, XXIV (Aug. 1), 175.
C835 "New Novels" [R.], *Listener*, XXIV (Aug. 15), 247.
C836 "New Novels" [R.], *Listener*, XXIV (Aug. 29), 319.
C837 "Then" [P.], *Poetry*, LVI (Sept.), 311.
C838 "New Novels" [R., incl. Robert Graves, *Sergeant Lamb of the
Ninth*], *Listener*, XXIV (Sept. 19), 427.
C839 "New Novels" [R.], *Listener*, XXIV (Oct. 3), 495.
C840 "The Writer and His Public: Part of a Discussion between V. S.
Pritchett, Edwin Muir, and Desmond Hawkins" [Broadcast], *Lis-
tener*, XXIV (Oct. 17), 557-58.
C841 "New Novels" [R.], *Listener*, XXIV (Oct. 24), 603.
C842 "New Novels" [R., incl. William Faulkner, *The Hamlet*], *Listener*,
XXIV (Nov. 14), 711.
C843 "New Novels" [R.], *Listener*, XXIV (Nov. 28), 782.
C844 "New Novels" [R.], *Listener*, XXIV (Dec. 12), 852.
C845 "The Leaning Tower" [R., *Folios of New Writing, II*], *New S*, XX
(Dec. 21), 656.
C846 "New Novels" [R.], *Listener*, XXIV (Dec. 26), 920.

1941

C847 "New Novels" [R., incl. Arthur Koestler, *Darkness at Noon*], *Listener*, XXV (Jan. 16), 99.
C848 "The Grove" [P.], *New Alliance*, II (Feb.-March), 11.

C849 "New Novels" [R.], *Listener*, XXV (Feb. 6), 207.

C850 "New Novels" [R.], *Listener*, XXV (Feb. 27), 314.

C851 "New Novels" [R., incl. Robert Graves, *Proceed, Sergeant Lamb*], *Listener*, XXV (March 13), 386.

C852 "Poem" ["Here at the wayside station"], *Listener*, XXV (March 20), 411.

C853 "New Novels" [R., incl. Ernest Hemingway, *For Whom the Bell Tolls*], *Listener*, XXV (March 27), 460.

C854 "Scotland, 1941" [P.], *New Alliance*, II (April-May), 9.

C855 "New Novels" [R.], *Listener*, XXV (April 17), 571.

C856 "Yeats" [R., Louis MacNeice, *Poetry of W. B. Yeats*], *New S*, XXI (April 26), 440.

C857 "New Novels" [R.], *Listener*, XXV (May 15), 709.

C858 "New Novels" [R.], *Listener*, XXV (May 22), 743.

C859 "The Obscure Image" [R.], *New S*, XXI (May 31), 558.

C860 "New Novels" [R., incl. I. Compton-Burnett, *Parents and Children*], *Listener*, XXV (June 5), 815.

C861 "New Novels" [R.], *Listener*, XXV (June 19), 887.

C862 "New Novels" [R.], *Listener*, XXVI (July 10), 67.

C863 "The Finder Found" [P.], *Spec*, No. 5898 (July 11), p. 33.

C864 "The Guess" [P.], *Spec*, No. 5899 (July 18), p. 57.

C865 "To J. F. H. (1897-1934)" [P.], *Listener*, XXVI (July 24), 116.

C866 "Virginia Woolf's Last Novel" [R., Virginia Woolf, *Between the Acts*], *Listener*, XXVI (July 24), 139.

C867 "Immortals" [R.], *New S*, XXII (July 26), 92-93.

C868 "New Novels" [R.], *Listener*, XXVI (July 31), 175.

C869 "To the Old Gods" [P.], *New Alliance*, II (Aug.-Sept.), 7.

C870 "The Status of the Novel" [E.], *New Republic*, CV (Aug. 11), 193-95.

C871 "The Recurrence. The Grove. The Finder Found" [P.], *Poetry* (Chicago), LVIII (Sept.), 320-23.

C872 "New Novels" [R.], *Listener*, XXVI (Aug. 14), 243.

C873 "New Novels" [R.], *Listener*, XXVI (Aug. 28), 315.

C874 "New Novels" [R.], *Listener*, XXVI (Sept. 18), 414.

C875 "New Novels" [R.], *Listener*, XXVI (Oct. 2), 478.

C876 "New Novels" [R.], *Listener*, XXVI (Oct. 16), 542.

C877 "The Prize" [P.], *Listener*, XXVI (Oct. 30), 586.

C878 "New Novels" [R.], *Listener*, XXVI (Oct. 30), 607.

C879 "New Novels" [R.], *Listener*, XXVI (Nov. 20), 702.

C880 "New Novels" [R.], *Listener*, XXVI (Dec. 11), 799.
C881 "The Trophy" [P.], *Listener*, XXVI (Dec. 18), 811.
C882 "New Novels" [R.], *Listener*, XXVI (Dec. 24), 682.
C883 "The Ring" [P.], *Spec*, No. 5922 (Dec. 26), p. 596.

1942

C884 "New Novels" [R.], *Listener*, XXVII (Jan. 15), 90.
C885 "New Novels" [R.], *Listener*, XXVII (Jan. 29), 155.
C886 "New Verse" [R.], *New S*, XXIII (Jan. 31), 80-81.
C887 "New Novels" [R.], *Listener*, XXVII (Feb. 12), 219.
C888 "Our Finest Love Poet Since Donne" [Broadcast talk about Brown-
       ing], *Listener*, XXVII (Feb. 26), 277-78.
C889 "New Novels" [R.], *Listener*, XXVII (March 5), 314.
C890 "New Novels" [R.], *Listener*, XXVII (March 19), 378.
C891 "New Novels" [R., incl. J. P. Marquand, *H. M. Pulham, Esq.*], *Lis-
       tener*, XXVII (April 2), 443.
C892 "New Novels" [R.], *Listener*, XXVII (April 23), 539.
C893 "New Novels" [R.], *Listener*, XXVII (May 7), 602.
C894 "New Novels" [R.], *Listener*, XXVII (May 28), 699.
C895 "The Swimmer's Death" [P.], *Listener*, XXVII (June 11), 742.
C896 "New Novels" [R., incl. Carson McCullers, *Reflections in a Golden
       Eye*], *Listener*, XXVII (June 18), 795.
C897 "The Natural Man and the Political Man" [E.], *New Writing and
       Daylight*, Summer, pp. 7-15.
C898 "New Novels" [R.], *Listener*, XXVIII (July 9), 59.
C899 "New Novels" [R.], *Listener*, XXVIII (July 23), 123.
C900 "The Face" [P.], *Listener*, XXVIII (July 30), 149.
C901 "The Wheel" [P.], *New Alliance*, III (Aug.-Sept.), 3.
C902 "New Novels" [R.], *Listener*, XXVIII (Aug. 13), 218.
C903 "New Novels" [R.], *Listener*, XXVIII (Aug. 27), 282.
C904 "The Admirable Crichton" [Broadcast talk], *Listener*, XXVIII
       (Sept. 3), 309-10.
C905 "New Novels" [R.], *Listener*, XXVIII (Sept. 17), 379.
C906 "New Novels" [R.], *Listener*, XXVIII (Oct. 1), 443.
C907 "New Novels" [R.], *Listener*, XXVIII (Oct. 15), 507.

C908 "New Novels" [R.], *Listener*, XXVIII (Oct. 29), 571.
C909 "New Novels" [R.], *Listener*, XXVIII (Nov. 19), 667.
C910 "New Novels" [R., incl. Joyce Cary, *To Be a Pilgrim*], *Listener*, XXVIII (Dec. 17), 795.

1943

C911 "New Novels" [R., incl. William Faulkner, *Go Down Moses*], *Listener*, XXIX (Jan. 14), 59.
C912 "New Novels" [R., incl. Evelyn Waugh, *Work Suspended*], *Listener*, XXIX (Feb. 4), 154.
C913 "Little Gidding" [R., T. S. Eliot, *Little Gidding*], *New S*, XXV (Feb. 20), 128.
C914 "New Novels" [R.], *Listener*, XXIX (Feb. 25), 250.
C915 "New Short Stories" [R.], *Listener*, XXIX (March 11), 310.
C916 "New Novels" [R.], *Listener*, XXIX (March 25), 370.
C917 "To Ann Scott-Moncrieff (1914-1943)" [P.], *New Alliance*, IV (April-May), 7.
C918 "New Novels" [R.], *Listener*, XXIX (April 15), 458.
C919 "New Novels" [R.], *Listener*, XXIX (May 6), 546.
C920 "New Novels" [R.], *Listener*, XXIX (May 27), 638.
C921 "New Novels" [R., incl. Graham Greene, *The Ministry of Fear*], *Listener*, XXIX (June 17), 730.
C922 "A Note on the English Romantic Movement," *Review-43*, I (Summer), 73-75.
C923 "Reading" [P.], *Listener*, XXX (July 8), 40.
C924 "New Novels" [R.], *Listener*, XXX (July 15), 78.
C925 "New Novels" [R.], *Listener*, XXX (July 29), 134.
C926 "New Novels" [R., incl. Eudora Welty, *A Curtain of Green*], *Listener*, XXX (Aug. 16), 218.
C927 "Poetry of Robert Frost" [R., Robert Frost, *Collected Poems* and *A Witness Tree*], *Listener*, XXX (Aug. 26), 246.
C928 "From a Diary," *New Alliance*, IV (Sept.-Oct.), 6-7.
C929 "New Novels" [R.], *Listener*, XXX (Sept. 16), 330.
C930 "New Novels" [R.], *Listener*, XXX (Sept. 30), 386.
C931 "New Novels" [R.], *Listener*, XXX (Oct. 28), 506.
C932 "New Short Stories" [R.], *Listener*, XXX (Nov. 18), 590.
C933 "To the Old Gods. The Trophy" [P.], *Poetry* (Chicago), LXIII (Dec.), 146-47.

C934 "New Novels" [R.], *Listener*, XXX (Dec. 9), 674.
C935 "New Novels" [R.], *Listener*, XXX (Dec. 30), 762.

1944

C936 "W. B. Yeats" [E. in French, trans. Austin and Madelaine Gill], *Fontaine* (Algiers), Nos. 37-40 ("Aspects de la littérature anglaise de 1918 à 1940"), pp. 106-15.
C937 "New Novels" [R.], *Listener*, XXXI (Jan. 20), 82.
C938 "New Novels" [R., incl. I. Compton-Burnett, *Elders and Betters*], *Listener*, XXXI (Feb. 10), 166.
C939 "New Short Stories" [R., incl. Virginia Woolf, *A Haunted House*], *Listener*, XXXI (March 2), 250.
C940 "New Novels" [R.], *Listener*, XXXI (March 16), 306.
C941 "New Novels" [R., incl. Katherine Butler Hathaway, *The Little Locksmith*], *Listener*, XXXI (April 6), 390.
C942 "New Novels" [R.], *Listener*, XXXI (April 20), 446.
C943 "New Novels" [R.], *Listener*, XXXI (May 11), 530.
C944 "New Novels" [R.], *Listener*, XXXI (June 1), 614.
C945 "New Novels" [R.], *Listener*, XXXI (June 15), 670.
C946 "New Novels" [R.], *Listener*, XXXII (July 6), 22.
C947 "New Novels" [R., incl. W. S. Maugham, *The Razor's Edge*], *Listener*, XXXII (July 27), 106.
C948 "New Novels" [R.], *Listener*, XXXII (Aug. 17), 190.
C949 "New Novels" [R.], *Listener*, XXXII (Sept. 14), 302.
C950 "New Novels" [R., incl. Joyce Cary, *The Horse's Mouth*], *Listener*, XXXII (Oct. 5), 386.
C951 "New Novels" [R., incl. Rosamond Lehmann, *The Ballad and the Source*], *Listener*, XXXII (Oct. 26), 470.
C952 "New Novels" [R.], *Listener*, XXXII (Nov. 16), 554.
C953 "New Novels" [R.], *Listener*, XXXII (Dec. 7), 637.
C954 "New Novels" [R.], *Listener*, XXXII (Dec. 28), 722.

1945

C955 "The Escape" [P.], *Listener*, XXXIII (Jan. 4), 12.
C956 "New Novels" [R.], *Listener*, XXXIII (Jan. 18), 78.
C957 "New Novels" [R.], *Listener*, XXXIII (Feb. 8), 162.

C958 "New Novels" [R.], *Listener*, XXXIII (March 1), 246.

C959 "New Novels" [R.], *Listener*, XXXIII (March 22), 330.

C960 "The Myth. The Fathers" [P.], *Orion*, I (Spring), 41-42.

C961 "New Novels" [R.], *Listener*, XXXIII (April 5), 386.

C962 "New Novels" [R.], *Listener*, XXXIII (April 26), 470.

C963 "New Novels" [R., incl. Eudora Welty, *The Wide Net*], *Listener*, XXXIII (May 24), 582.

C964 "New Novels" [R.], *Listener*, XXXIII (June 7), 638.

C965 "On Seeing Two Lovers in the Street" [P.], *Listener*, XXXIII (June 28), 706.

C966 "New Novels" [R., incl. Evelyn Waugh, *Brideshead Revisited*], *Listener*, XXXIII (June 28), 722.

C967 "New Novels" [R.], *Listener*, XXXIV (July 19), 78.

C968 "The Transmutation" [P.], *Listener*, XXXIV (July 26), 96.

C969 "New Novels" [R.], *Listener*, XXXIV (Aug. 9), 162.

C970 "Walter Scott" [Lecture], *University of Edinburgh Jnl*, XIII (Autumn), 79-88.
Reprinted *Sir Walter Scott Lectures*, intro. W. L. Renwick. Edinburgh, 1950.

C971 "New Novels" [R.], *Listener*, XXXIV (Sept. 6), 274.
A note on this page announces Muir's departure from England and points out that this is the last of the reviews which began in 1933 (C418).

C972 "The Voyage" [P.], *Orion*, II (Autumn), 7-9.

C973 " 'Royal Man:' Notes on the Tragedies of George Chapman" [E.], *Orion*, II (Autumn), 92-100.

C974 "The Castle" [P.], *Listener*, XXXIV (Nov. 8), 520.

C975 "Moses" [P.], *Listener*, XXXIV (Nov. 22), 586.

1947

C976 "The Way" [P.], *Listener*, XXXVII (March 6), 334.

C977 "The Labyrinth" [P.], *Listener*, XXXVII (March 20), 432.

C978 "Sonnet" ["No, no, I did not bargain for so much"], *Listener*, XXXVII (April 24), 623.

C979 "Father and Son" [R., Max Brod, *Kafka, A Biography*, trans. G. H. Roberts], *Listener*, XXXVII (May 1), 680.

C980 "Sonnet" ["I knew it, yes, before Time"], *Listener*, XXXVII (May 22), 791.

C981 "The Child Dying" [P.], *Listener*, XXXVII (June 26), 994.
C982 "The Combat" [P.], *Listener*, XXXVIII (Sept. 4), 386.
C983 "The Return" [P.], *Listener*, XXXVIII (Sept. 18), 479.
C984 "The Helmet" [P.], *Listener*, XXXVIII (Oct. 9), 625.
C985 "Oedipus" [P.], *Listener*, XXXVIII (Oct. 16), 681.
C986 "Soliloquy" [P.], *Listener*, XXXVIII (Oct. 30), 779.

1948

C987 "The Bridge of Dread" [P.], *Listener*, XXXIX (Jan. 1), 16.
C988 "The Toy Horse" [P.], *Listener*, XXXIX (Jan. 8), 59.
C989 "The Transfiguration" [P.], *Listener*, XXXIX (Feb. 19), 304.
C990 "The Usurpers" [P.], *Listener*, XL (July 1), 27.
C991 "The Journey Back" [P.], *Listener*, XL (Aug. 19), 279.
C992 "The Interrogation" [P.], *Listener*, XL (Sept. 2), 347.
C993 "The Good Town" [P.], *Listener*, XL (Nov. 25), 807.
C994 "A German Parable" [R., Ernst Kreuder, *The Attic Pretenders*, trans. Robert Kee], *Observer*, No. 8219 (Dec. 5), p. 3.

1949

C995 "The Days. The Animals" [P.], *Botteghe Oscure*, IV, 386-88.
C996 "Modern Poetry" [R., Cleanth Brooks, *Modern Poetry and the Tradition*; and F. O. Matthiessen, *The Achievement of T. S. Eliot*], *Observer*, No. 8223 (Jan. 9), p. 3.
      Cf. C572.
C997 "Modern Love" [R., George Meredith, *Modern Love*], *Observer*, No. 8224 (Jan. 16), p. 3.
C998 "Unhappy Families" [R., I. Compton-Burnett, *Men and Wives, More Women than Men*], *Observer*, No. 8226 (Jan. 30), p. 3.
C999 "M. Gide as Critic" [R., André Gide, *Dostoyevsky*], *Observer*, (Feb. 13), p. 3.
C1000 "Family Life" [R.], *Observer*, No. 8230 (Feb. 27), p. 3.
C1001 "War and Peace" [R., E. J. Simmons, *Leo Tolstoy*], *Observer*, No. 8233 (March 20), p. 3.
C1002 "Existentialism" [R., Paul Foulquié, *Existentialism*; Jean Paul Sartre, *Existentialism and Humanism*; Gabriel Marcel, *The Philosophy of Existence*], *Observer*, No. 8234 (March 27), p. 3.
C1003 "Old and New" [R., Lord David Cecil, *Poets and Storytellers*;

C. M. Bowra, *The Creative Experiment*], *Observer*, No. 8237 (April 17), p. 3.

C1004 "A New Faust" [R., Thomas Mann, *Dr. Faustus*], *Observer*, No. 8239 (May 1), p. 7.

C1005 "The End of an Era" [R., Osbert Sitwell, *Laughter in the Next Room*], *Observer*, No. 8243 (May 29), p. 7.

C1006 "Kafka Again" [R., Franz Kafka, *Diaries* (Vol. II) and Charles Neider, *Kafka: His Mind and Art*], *Observer*, No. 8245 (June 12), p. 7.

C1007 "The Usurpers. Song" ["Sunset ends the day"] [P.], *Virginia Qtly Rev*, XXV (July), 386-88.

C1008 "Modern Criticism" [R., W. H. Gardner, *Gerard Manley Hopkins* (Vol. II)], *Observer*, No. 8249 (July 10), p. 7.

C1009 "Robert Burns" [R., Hilton Brown, *There Was A Lad*], *Observer*, No. 8251 (July 24), p. 7.

C1010 "Jane Austen and the Sense of Evil" [E.], *New York Times Book Review*, LIV (Aug. 28), 1, 25.

C1011 "Man and Poet" [R., Albert Schweitzer, *Goethe*], *Observer*, No. 8256 (Aug. 28), p. 7.

C1012 "Poetic Method" [R., Cleanth Brooks, *The Well Wrought Urn*], *Observer*, No. 8258 (Sept. 11), p. 7.

C1013 "The Defeated" [R.], *Observer*, No. 8260 (Sept. 25), p. 7.

C1014 "The Man Pope" [R., Norman Ault, *New Light on Pope*], *Observer*, No. 8261 (Oct. 2), p. 7.

C1015 "Edgar Allan Poe" [R., *The Centenary Poe*, ed. Montagu Slater; N. Bryllion Fagin, *The Histrionic Mr. Poe*], *Observer*, No. 8263 (Oct. 16), p. 7.

C1016 "Poetry's Slave" [R., Nora Wydenbruck, *Rilke: Man and Poet*], *Observer*, No. 8270 (Dec. 4), p. 7.

C1017 "Double Vision" [R., Kathleen Raine, *The Pythoness*], *Observer*, No. 8272 (Dec. 18), p. 7.

C1018 "Night and Day" [P.], *Listener*, XLII (Dec. 29), 1142.

1950

C1019 "The Shrine. The Son. The Late Wasp" [P.], *Botteghe Oscure*, V, 307-10.

C1020 "Between the Lines" [R., Richard Ellmann, *Yeats*; and D. A. Stauffer, *The Golden Nightingale*], *Observer*, No. 8274 (Jan. 1), p. 7.

C1021 "Good Criticism" [R., Edward Sackville West, *Inclinations*], *Observer*, No. 8276 (Jan. 15), p. 7.

C1022 "Natural Magic" [R.], *Observer*, No. 8279 (Feb. 5), p. 7.

C1023 "A Born Writer" [R.], *Observer*, No. 8281 (Feb. 19), p. 7.

C1024 "A German Diary" [R.], *Observer*, No. 8283 (March 5), p. 7.

C1025 "A Great Novelist" [R., René Béhaine, *Day of Glory*, trans. Bernard Miall], *Observer*, No. 8285 (March 19), p. 7.

C1026 "Common Sense" [R.], *Observer*, No. 8286 (March 26), p. 9.

C1027 "Ordinary Lives" [R., Antonia White, *The Lost Traveller*], *Observer*, No. 8289 (April 16), p. 7.

C1028 "W. H. Auden" [R., W. H. Auden, *Collected Shorter Poems*], *Observer*, No. 8291 (April 30), p. 7.

C1029 "Loss and Gain" [P.], *Listener*, XLIII (May 25), 924.

C1030 "Late Romantics" [R., J. F. Heath-Stubbs, *The Darkling Plain*], *Observer*, No. 8296 (June 4), p. 7.

C1031 "Wordsworth the Poet" [E.], *Observer*, No. 8298 (June 18), p. 7.

C1032 "From a Roman Bas-Relief. The Mediterranean Island" [P.], *Botteghe Oscure*, VI, 330-32.

C1033 "The New Literature" [R., Jean Paul Sartre, *What Is Literature?*], *Observer*, No. 8300 (July 2), p. 7.

C1034 "The Other Story" [P.], *Listener*, XLIV (July 6), 26.

C1035 "The Creative Act" [R., Leone Vivante, *English Poetry*], *Observer*, No. 8302 (July 16), p. 7.

C1036 "A Modern Fable" [R.], *Observer*, No. 8304 (July 30), p. 7.

C1037 "Nonconformist" [R., J. H. Hanford, *John Milton*], *Observer*, No. 8307 (Aug. 20), p. 7.

C1038 "An Original Writer" [R., Kay Cicellis, *The Easy Way*], *Observer*, No. 8309 (Sept. 3), p. 7.

C1039 "Adam's Dream" [P.], *Listener*, XLIV (Sept. 14), 352.

C1040 "Vintage Essays" [R.], *Observer*, No. 8311 (Sept. 17), p. 7.

C1041 "Dostoevsky" [R.], *Observer*, No. 8312 (Sept. 24), p. 7.

C1042 "The Closed Ring" [R.], *Observer*, No. 8313 (Oct. 1), p. 7.

C1043 "Human Freedom" [R.], *Observer*, No. 8315 (Oct. 15), p. 7.

C1044 "The Succession" [P.], *Listener*, XLIV (Nov. 2), 457.

C1045 "All in Focus" [R., Geoffrey Grigson, *The Crest on the Silver*], *Observer*, No. 8319 (Nov. 12), p. 7.

C1046 *"Don Quixote"* [R., translation by J. M. Cohen], *Observer*, No. 8321 (Nov. 26), p. 7.

C1047 "David Gascoyne" [R., David Gascoyne, *A Vagrant and Other Poems*], *Observer*, No. 8325 (Dec. 25), p. 7.

1951

C1048 "American Poetry" [R., *The Oxford Book of American Verse*, ed. F. O. Matthiessen; and Robert Lowell, *Poems*], *Observer*, No. 8328 (Jan. 14), p. 7.

C1049 "The Italian Spirit" [R., *Anthology of New Italian Writers*, ed. Marguerite Caetani], *Observer*, No. 8331 (Feb. 4), p. 7.

C1050 "The Dark Vision" [R.], *Observer*, No. 8333 (Feb. 18), p. 7.

C1051 "Herman Melville" [R., Herman Melville, *Complete Short Stories*, ed. J. Leyda], *Observer*, No. 8335 (March 4), p. 7.

C1052 "The Romantic Sea" [R., W. H. Auden, *The Enchafèd Flood*], *Observer*, No. 8337 (March 18), p. 7.

C1053 "Illumination" [R., Graham Greene, *The Lost Childhood*], *Observer*, No. 8339 (April 1), p. 7.

C1054 "A False Sunset?" [R., Arthur Koestler, *The Age of Longing*], *Observer*, No. 8341 (April 15), p. 7.

C1055 "The Gadget" [R.], *Observer*, No. 8344 (May 6), p. 7.

C1056 "The Types" [R.], *Observer*, No. 8345 (May 13), p. 7.

C1057 "Songs of the Soul" [R., *Poems of St. John of the Cross*, trans. Roy Campbell], *Observer*, No. 8347 (May 27), p. 7.

C1058 "The Decline of the Imagination" [Broadcast], *Listener*, XLV (May 10), 753-54.
Correspondence (May 17), 798; Muir's reply (May 24), 839-40.

C1059 "Eurydice" [P.], *Listener*, XLV (May 31), 863.

C1060 "Time's Wheels" [R., Walter de la Mare, *Winged Chariot*], *Observer*, No. 8351 (June 24), p. 7.

C1061 "A Rare Genius" [R., Hans Carossa, *The Year of Sweet Illusions*, trans. Robert Kee], *Observer*, No. 8352 (July 1), p. 7.

C1062 "A Strange Story" [R.], *Observer*, No. 8354 (July 15), p. 7.

C1063 "Within A Mystery" [R.], *Observer*, No. 8357 (Aug. 5), p. 7.

C1064 "Two Voices" [R.], *Observer*, No. 8358 (Aug. 12), p. 7.

C1065 "Crude Genius" [R., F. O. Matthiessen, *Theodore Dreiser*], *Observer*, No. 8360 (Aug. 26), p. 7.

C1066 "The Charm" [P.], *Listener*, XLVI (Aug. 30), 336.

C1067 "Love and Hate" [R., Graham Greene, *The End of the Affair*], *Observer*, No. 8361 (Sept. 2), p. 7.

C1068 "Love and Poetry" [R., Rainer Maria Rilke, *Letters to Merline*], *Observer*, No. 8363 (Sept. 16), p. 7.

C1069 "Sonnet," *Listener*, XLVI (Sept. 27), 515.
C1070 "Two Poets" [R., *Complete Poems of Emily Brontë*; Marianne Moore, *Collected Poems*], *Observer*, No. 8365 (Sept. 30), p. 7.
C1071 "Critics' Choice" [R.], *Observer*, No. 8367 (Oct. 14), p. 7.
C1072 "A Comic Figure" [R.], *Observer*, No. 8368 (Oct. 21), p. 7.
C1073 "To Franz Kafka" [P.], *Listener*, XLVI (Nov. 1), 759.
C1074 "The Missing Cheer" [R., E. M. Forster, *Two Cheers for Democracy*], *Observer*, No. 8370 (Nov. 4), p. 7.
C1075 "Rose and Worm" [R.], *Observer*, No. 8373 (Nov. 25), p. 7.
C1076 "The Island. The Animals. Night and Day. The Succession" [P.], *Hudson Rev*, IV (Winter), 512.
C1077 "A New Writer" [R.], *Observer*, No. 8374 (Dec. 2), p. 7.
C1078 "Sonnet," *Listener*, XLVI (Dec. 6), 964.
C1079 "The Late Swallow" [P.], *Listener*, XLVI (Dec. 13), 1025.
C1080 "The Professional" [R.], *Observer*, No. 8376 (Dec. 16), p. 7.

1952

C1081 "Sonnet" ["The great road stretched before us, clear and still."], *Listener*, XLVII (Jan. 3), 8.
C1082 "Cats and Dogs" [R., Colette, *Creatures Great and Small*], *Observer*, No. 8379 (Jan. 6), p. 7.
C1083 "True Judgment" [R., F. R. Leavis, *The Common Pursuit*], *Observer*, No. 8381 (Jan. 20), p. 7.
C1084 "For Enjoyment" [R.], *Observer*, No. 8383 (Feb. 3), p. 7.
C1085 "Miss Mansfield" [R., Sylvia Berkman, *Katherine Mansfield*], *Observer*, No. 8385 (Feb. 17), p. 7.
C1086 "Making Friends" [R., Rupert Hart-Davis, *Hugh Walpole*], *Observer*, No. 8388 (March 9), p. 7.
C1087 "The Robber" [R.], *Observer*, No. 8390 (March 23), p. 7.
C1088 "Helpless Greatness" [R.], *Observer*, No. 8392 (April 6), p. 7.
C1089 "What Man Is" [R.], *Observer*, No. 8394 (April 20), p. 7.
C1090 "Sonnet" ["Nothing, it seemed, between them and the grave"], *New S*, XLIII (May 3), 529.
C1091 "The Fatal Chain" [R., Thomas Mann, *The Holy Sinner*, trans. H. T. Lowe-Porter], *Observer*, No. 8396 (May 4), p. 7.
C1092 "Island in the Sun" [R.], *Observer*, No. 8397 (May 11), p. 7.
C1093 "Metamorphoses" [R., John Lehmann, *The Open Night*], *Observer*, No. 8399 (May 25), p. 7.
C1094 "European Writing" [R., *Botteghe Oscure* (IX)], *Observer*, No. 8400 (June 1), p. 7.

C1095 "The Killing. The Betrayer. The Choice" [P.], *Botteghe Oscure*, IX, 156-58.

C1096 "The Other Oedipus" [P.], *New S*, XLIII (June 14), 706.

C1097 "A Pantheist" [R., Llewelyn Powys, *A Selection*, ed. Kenneth Hopkins], *Observer*, No. 8402 (June 15), p. 7.

C1098 "A Sad Spectacle" [R., A. C. Swinburne, *Lesbia Brandon*], *Observer*, No. 8404 (June 29), p. 7.

C1099 "The Damned" [R., Angus Wilson, *Hemlock and After*], *Observer*, No. 8406 (July 13), p. 7.

C1100 "Antichrist" [P.], *Listener*, XLVIII (July 17), 99.

C1101 "Parturiunt Montes" [R., *Selections . . . Thomas Wolfe*, ed M. Geismar], *Observer*, No. 8410 (Aug. 10), p. 7.

C1102 "Reading Poems" [R., Rosemond Tuve, *A Reading of George Herbert*], *Observer*, No. 8412 (Aug. 24), p. 7.

C1103 "Two Novelists" [R., Evelyn Waugh, *Men at Arms*; Ernest Hemingway, *The Old Man and the Sea*], *Observer*, No. 8414 (Sept. 7), p. 7.

C1104 "The Real R. L. S." [R.], *Observer*, No. 8416 (Sept. 21), p. 9.

C1105 "Hölderlin" [R., *Hölderlin, His Poems*, trans. Michael Hamburger; L. S. Salzberger, *Hölderlin*], *Observer*, No. 8419 (Oct. 12), p. 11.

C1106 "Shakespeare's Heroes" [P.], *New S*, XLIV (Oct. 18), 454.

C1107 "A Great Austrian" [R., *Selected Prose of Hugo von Hofmannsthal*], *Observer*, No. 8420 (Oct. 19), p. 8.

C1108 "Correspondences" [R.], *Observer*, No. 8422 (Nov. 2), p. 9.

C1109 "Private Life" [R.], *Observer*, No. 8424 (Nov. 16), p. 9.

C1110 "Uncle Arnold" [R., Reginald Pound, *Arnold Bennett*], *Observer*, No. 8426 (Nov. 30), p. 9.

C1111 "Song" ["This will not pass so soon"], *Listener*, XLVIII (Dec. 4), 932.

C1112 "What's Wrong" [R.], *Observer*, No. 8428 (Dec. 14), p. 9.

C1113 "The Year's Christmas" [P.], *Observer*, No. 8429 (Dec. 21), p. 7.

C1114 "Twenties and Thirties" [R., Edmund Wilson, *The Shores of Light*], *Observer*, No. 8430 (Dec. 28), p. 7.

1953

C1115 "Younger Poets" [R., *Poems in Pamphlet* (various issues), ed. Erica Marx], *Observer*, No. 8432 (Jan. 11), p. 7.

C1116 "The Young Princes" [P.], *Listener*, XLIX (Feb. 19), 296.

C1117 "Introducing Musil" [R., Robert Musil, *A Man Without Quali-ties*, trans. E. Wilkins and E. Kaiser], *Observer*, No. 8440 (March 8), p. 11.
Cf. C1151.

C1118 "Family Relations" [R., I. Compton-Burnett, *The Present and the Past*], *Observer*, No. 8442 (March 22), p. 9.

C1119 "Song" ["This that I give and take"], *Listener*, XLIX (March 26), 506.

C1120 "Maxim Gorki" [R.], *Observer*, No. 8444 (April 5), p. 7.

C1121 "Enfant Terrible" [R., Wallace Fowlie, *Rimbaud's Illuminations*], *Observer*, No. 8447 (April 26), p. 9.

C1122 "Wish-Fulfilment" [R.], *Observer*, No. 8449 (May 10), p. 11.

C1123 "Newbattle Abbey" [P.], *New S*, XLV (May 23), 618.

C1124 "Probing in Vain" [R.], *Observer*, No. 8453 (June 7), p. 9.

C1125 "Telemachos Remembers" [P.], *Listener*, XLIX (June 18), 1011.

C1126 "The Northern Islands" [P.], *New S*, XLV (June 20), 738.

C1127 "Old Vienna" [R.], *Observer*, No. 8455 (June 21), p. 11.

C1128 "Words, Words" [R., Mario Pei, *The Story of English*], *Observer*, No. 8457 (July 5), p. 9.

C1129 "Kafka Speaks" [R., Gustav Janouch, *Conversations with Kafka*, trans. Goronwy Rees], *Observer*, No. 8459 (July 19), p. 9.

C1130 "Dream and Thing" [P.], *Listener*, L (July 30), 178.

C1131 "New Poems for Old" [R., *The Translations of Ezra Pound*], *Observer*, No. 8461 (Aug. 2), p. 7.

C1132 "Christian Humanism" [R., Jacques Maritain, *The Range of Reason*], *Observer*, No. 8463 (Aug. 16), p. 7.

C1133 "The Learned Knife" [R., *Franz Kafka: Letters to Milena*, ed. Willi Haas, trans. Tania and James Stern], *Observer*, No. 8465 (Aug. 30), p. 7.

C1134 "The W. E. A." [E.], *Observer*, No. 8466 (Sept. 6), p. 8.

C1135 "Modern Poetry" [R., *The Faber Book of Twentieth-Century Verse*, ed. J. F. Heath-Stubbs and David Wright], *Observer*, No. 8467 (Sept. 13), p. 9.

C1136 "The Dickens Question" [R.], *Observer*, No. 8469 (Sept. 27), p. 11.

C1137 "Ketman in Action" [R.], *Observer*, No. 8471 (Oct. 11), p. 11.

C1138 "Character" [R.], *Observer*, No. 8473 (Oct. 25), p. 11.

C1139 "Two Sonnets" ["You through whom we have lost and still shall lose" and "They could not tell me who should be my lord"], *Partisan Rev*, XX (Nov.), 634.

C1140 "The Gods Under Fire" [R.], *Observer*, No. 8475 (Nov. 8), p. 8.

C1141 "Dylan Thomas" [Obituary notice], *Observer*, No. 8476 (Nov. 15), p. 10.

C1142 "In the Family" [R.], *Observer*, No. 8477 (Nov. 22), p. 9.

C1143 "Visionaries" [R., Stephen Spender, *The Creative Element*], *Observer*, No. 8479 (Dec. 6), p. 9.

C1144 "Two Lives" [R.], *Observer*, No. 8481 (Dec. 20), p. 7.

1954

C1145 "For Reference" [R.], *Observer*, No. 8483 (Jan. 3), p. 7.

C1146 "The Combat" [P.], *Listener*, LI (Jan. 14), 103.

C1147 "Mrs. Isabella Jones" [R., Robert Gittings, *John Keats: The Living Year*], *Observer*, No. 8485 (Jan. 17), p. 9.

C1148 "Critics and Laymen" [R., G. M. Trevelyan, *A Layman's Love of Letters*], *Observer*, No. 8487 (Jan. 31), p. 9.

C1149 "A Ticket to Paradise" [R., Aldous Huxley, *The Doors of Perception*], *Observer*, No. 8489 (Feb. 14), p. 9.

C1150 "Hyperbolist" [R.], *Observer*, No. 8492 (March 7), p. 9.

C1151 "Innovator" [R., Robert Musil, *The Man Without Qualities*, II, trans. E. Wilkins and E. Kaiser], *Observer*, No. 8494 (March 21), p. 9.
Cf. C1117.

C1152 "The Incarnate One" [P.], *Saltire Rev*, I (April), 7.

C1153 "The Great Dean" [R., J. Middleton Murry, *Jonathan Swift*], *Observer*, No. 8496 (April 4), p. 9.

C1154 "The Enchanter" [R., *Selected Works of Rilke*, trans. G. C. Houston], *Observer*, No. 8498 (April 18), p. 7.

C1155 "Sonnet; Two Songs" [P.], *Hudson Rev*, VII (Spring), 49-50.

C1156 "Dresden, Hellerau, and Vienna—A Memoir" [E.], *Encounter*, II (May), 36-43.

C1157 "Tolstoy Again" [R.], *Observer*, No. 8500 (May 2), p. 9.

C1158 "George Herbert" [R., J. H. Summers, *George Herbert*; Margaret Bottrall, *George Herbert*], *Observer*, No. 8502 (May 16), p. 11.

C1159 "A Study of Bloomsbury" [R., J. K. Johnstone, *The Bloomsbury Group*], *Observer*, No. 8504 (May 30), p. 9.

C1160 "A False Move" [R., Christopher Isherwood, *The World in the Evening*], *Observer*, No. 8507 (June 20), p. 9.

C1161 "Private Worlds" [R., Bonamy Dobrée, *The Broken Cistern*], *Observer*, No. 8509 (July 4), p. 11.

C1162 "Sonnet" ["However it came, this great house has gone down"], *Listener*, LII (July 15), 87.

C1163 "The Scorpion" [R., Marion Lochhead, *John Gibson Lockhart*], *Observer*, No. 8512 (July 25), p. 9.

C1164 "Experimental" [R.], *Observer*, No. 8514 (Aug. 8), p. 7.

C1165 "Strange Epic" [R., J. R. R. Tolkien, *The Fellowship of the Ring*], *Observer*, No. 8516 (Aug. 22), p. 7.
       Cf. C1172, C1200.

C1166 "Imprisoned" [R., Franz Kafka, *Wedding Preparations*, trans. E. Kaiser and E. Wilkins], *Observer*, No. 8518 (Sept. 5), p. 11.

C1167 "Indirections" [R.], *Observer*, No. 8520 (Sept. 19), p. 13.

C1168 "Some Conclusions" [E.], *Observer*, No. 8521 (Sept. 26), p. 8.

C1169 "Ghost Voices" [R.], *Observer*, No. 8522 (Oct. 3), p. 9.

C1170 "Wordsworth" [R., F. W. Bateson, *Wordsworth: A Reinterpretation*], *Observer*, No. 8524 (Oct. 17), p. 9.

C1171 "Western Ways" [R.], *Observer*, No. 8528 (Nov. 14), p. 9.

C1172 "The Ring" [R., J. R. R. Tolkien, *The Two Towers*], *Observer*, No. 8529 (Nov. 21), p. 9.
       Cf. C1165.

C1173 "Effigies" [P.], *New S*, XLVIII (Nov. 27), 712.

C1174 "Portrait of a Storyteller" [R., Hesketh Pearson, *Walter Scott*], *Listener*, LII (Dec. 2), 981.

C1175 "Poets of Two Ages" [R., C. Day Lewis, *Collected Poems*; Frances Cornford, *Collected Poems*], *Observer*, No. 8531 (Dec. 5), p. 9.

C1176 "Ways of Fame" [R.], *Observer*, No. 8533 (Dec. 19), p. 11.

1955

C1177 "The Grave of Prometheus" [P.], *Listener*, LIII (Jan. 13), 67.

C1178 "The Picturesque" [R.], *Observer*, No. 8537 (Jan. 16), p. 9.

C1179 "Abraham" [P.], *Listener*, LIII (Jan. 27), 158.

C1180 "Poet's Progress" [R., Stephen Spender, *Collected Poems*], *Observer*, No. 8539 (Jan. 30), p. 9.

C1181 "Passions Imprisoned" [R., I. Compton-Burnett, *Mother and Son*; Robert Liddell, *The Novels of Ivy Compton-Burnett*], *Observer*, No. 8540 (Feb. 6), p. 9.

C1182 "Sister Benedicta" [R.], *Observer*, No. 8542 (Feb. 20), p. 11.

C1183 "Odes from the East" [R., Ezra Pound, *The Classic Anthology*;

J. J. Espey, *Ezra Pound's Mauberley*], *Observer*, No. 8544 (March 6), p. 9.

C1184 "The Horses" [P.], *Listener*, LIII (March 10), 429.

C1185 "The Curé of Meudon" [R., *Gargantua and Pantagruel*, trans. J. M. Cohen], *Observer*, No. 8546 (March 20), p. 9.

C1186 "Thou Art Translated" [R., *Selected Fables of La Fontaine*, trans. Marianne Moore], *Observer*, No. 8547 (April 24), p. 14.

C1187 "The Poor Critic" [R., Harold Osborne, *Aesthetics and Criticism*], *Observer*, No. 8548 (May 1), p. 17.

C1188 "New Utopias" [R.], *Observer*, No. 8550 (May 15), p. 17.

C1189 "Existentialist Shudders" [R., *Kierkegaard*, intro. W. H. Auden; Arland Ussher, *Journey Through Dread*], *Observer*, No. 8551 (May 22), p. 17.

C1190 "A New Writer" [R.], *Observer*, No. 8553 (June 5), p. 7.

C1191 "The Wide View" [R., C. M. Bowra, *Inspiration and Poetry*], *Observer*, No. 8555 (June 19), p. 13.

C1192 "The Moment. The Cloud. The Difficult Land" [P.], *Botteghe Oscure*, XV, 88-92.

C1193 "A Practical Man" [R.], *Observer*, No. 8559 (July 17), p. 9.

C1194 "What Is Contemporary?" [R., Stephen Spender, *The Making of a Poem*], *Observer*, No. 8561 (July 31), p. 7.

C1195 "Thoughts on Meredith" [R., *Selected Poetical Works of George Meredith*, compiled by G. M. Trevelyan], *Observer*, No. 8563 (Aug. 14), p. 9.

C1196 "Piling it On" [R., Heinrich Heine, *The North Sea*, trans. Vernon Watkins], *Observer*, No. 8565 (Aug. 28), p. 9.

C1197 "The Muse and the Market Place" [R., Robert Graves, *The Crowning Privilege*; Malcolm Cowley, *The Literary Situation*], *Observer*, No. 8572 (Oct. 16), p. 12.

C1198 "The Last Laugh" [R.], *Observer*, No. 8574 (Oct. 30), p. 13.

C1199 "Intellect and Imagination" [R., *Collected Poems of Wallace Stevens*], *Observer*, No. 8575 (Nov. 6), p. 10.

C1200 "A Boy's World" [R., J. R. R. Tolkien, *The Return of the Ring*], *Observer*, No. 8578 (Nov. 27), p. 11.
Cf. C1165.

C1201 "Images" [P.], *Encounter*, V (Dec.), 52.

C1202 "Book Choices of 1955," *Observer*, No. 8582 (Dec. 25), p. 7.
Muir's choices were Thomas Mann, *The Confessions of Felix Krull*; *Collected Poems of Wallace Stevens*; Norman McCaig, *Riding Lights*.

1956

C1203 "The Bad Lands" [P.], *Listener*, LV (Jan. 5), 15.

C1204 "Problems of Prosperity" [E.], *Observer*, No. 8588 (Feb. 5), p. 10.

C1205 "The American Writer" [R., Edmund Wilson, *The Shock of Recognition*], *Observer*, No. 8598 (April 15), p. 12.

C1206 "Complaint of the Dying Peasantry" [P.], *Saltire Rev*, III (Spring), 11.

C1207 "Evolution of Courtesy" [R., Harold Nicolson, *Good Behaviour*], *Nation* (NY), CLXXXII (May 5), 386.

C1208 "Recent American Poetry" [E.], *Observer*, No. 8601 (May 6), p. 17.

C1209 "Deep in Joyce" [R., Hugh Kenner, *Dublin's Joyce*], *Observer*, No. 8607 (June 17), p. 11.

C1210 "The Church" [P.], *Encounter*, VII (July), 55.

C1211 "Faith and Works" [R., *Craft of Letters in England*, ed. John Lehmann], *Observer*, No. 8610 (July 8), p. 9.

C1212 "Among the Lost" [R.], *Observer*, No. 8612 (July 22), p. 9.

C1213 "The Bildungsroman" [R.], *New S*, LII (Sept. 8), 286-87.

C1214 "In Search for a Synthesis" [R., Arnold Toynbee, *An Historian's Approach to Religion*], *Observer*, No. 8619 (Sept. 9), p. 13.

C1215 "A Country Tale" [P.], *New S*, LII (Oct. 6), 428.

C1216 "The American Short Story" [E.], *Observer*, No. 8623 (Oct. 7), p. 16.

C1217 "Neat, Muted and Despondent" [R., *Poetry Now*, ed. G. S. Fraser], *Observer*, No. 8624 (Oct. 14), p. 17.

C1218 "The Tower. The Two Sisters." [P.], *Nation* (NY), CLXXXIII (Nov. 10), 406, 409.

C1219 "Shelley Plainer" [R., Neville Rogers, *Shelley at Work*], *Observer*, No. 8628 (Nov. 11), p. 13.

C1220 "Profitable Indirections" [R., E. M. Butler, *Byron and Goethe* and *Heinrich Heine*], *New S*, LII (Dec. 1), 718.

C1221 "Crucial Questions" [R., Allen Tate, *The Man of Letters in the Modern World*], *Observer*, No. 8632 (Dec. 9), p. 13.

C1222 "Reports on Time: After 1984; The Strange Return" [P.], *New S*, LII (Dec. 22), 821.

C1223 "Books of the Year," *Observer*, No. 8634 (Dec. 23), p. 6.
Muir's choices were Kathleen Raine, *Collected Poems*; Allen Tate, *Man of Letters*; E. M. Butler, *Byron and Goethe*.

1957

C1224 "Chinese Numbers" [R.], *Observer*, No. 8637 (Jan. 13), p. 10.

C1225 "The New Illiteracy" [R., R. P. Blackmur, *The Lion and the Honeycomb*], *Observer*, No. 8640 (Feb. 3), p. 12.

C1226 "Ballads" [R., F. J. Child, *English and Scottish Popular Ballads*], *New S*, LIII (Feb. 9), 174-75.

C1227 "The Young Wordsworth" [R., Mary Moorman, *William Wordsworth*], *Observer*, No. 8642 (Feb. 17), p. 14.

C1228 "Excess and Measure" [R.], *New S*, LIII (March 2), 284.

C1229 "Secular Religion" [R., J. Middleton Murry, *Love, Freedom and Society*], *Observer*, No. 8645 (March 10), p. 16.

C1230 "Wise Bairn" [R., James Kirkup, *The Only Child*], *Listener*, LVII (March 14), 437.

C1231 "Something to be Thankful For" [R.], *New S*, LIII (April 6), 447-48.

C1232 "The Villain as Hero" [R., D. P. Varma, *The Gothic Flame*], *Observer*, No. 8650 (April 14), p. 16.

C1233 "Natural Goethe" [R.], *New S*, LIII (April 27), 545-46.

C1234 "Zarathustra" [R., F. A. Lea, *The Tragic Philosopher*], *Observer*, No. 8653 (May 5), p. 16.

C1235 "Fantasy and Reality" [R.], Observer, No. 8655 (May 19), p. 17.

C1236 "Strange Literature" [R.], *New S*, LIII (May 25), 680.

C1237 "The Fortified Eye" [R., Geoffrey Wagner, *Wyndham Lewis*], *Observer*, No. 8660 (June 23), p. 13.

C1238 "Three Tales. The Desolations. Salem, Massachusetts. The Brothers." [P.], *Botteghe Oscure*, XIX, 75-78.

C1239 "Time and Place" [R., incl. Edmund Blunden, *Poems of Many Years*], *New S*, LIV (July 13), 59-60.

C1240 "The Conqueror" [P.], *Listener*, LVIII (July 18), 99.

C1241 "Austrian Genius" [R., H. A. Hammelmann, *Hofmannsthal*], *Observer*, No. 8664 (July 21), p. 13.

C1242 "Empiric-Romantic" [R., Robert Langbaum, *The Poetry of Experience*], *Observer*, No. 8666 (Aug. 4), p. 8.

C1243 "Father and Clown" (R., I. Compton-Burnett, *A Father and His Fate*], *Observer*, No. 8667 (Aug. 11), p. 13.

C1244 "Two Critics" [R., Lionel Trilling, *A Gathering of Fugitives*; John Wain, *Preliminary Essays*], *Observer*, No. 8668 (Aug. 18), p. 12.

C1245 "A Personal Mythology" [R., George Barker, *Collected Poems* and *The True Confession of George Barker*], *New S*, LIV (Aug. 31), 252.

C1246 "Brave Old World" [R., Denis Saurat, *Atlantis and the Giants*], *Observer*, No. 8672 (Sept. 15), p. 14.

C1247 "Kinds of Poetry" [R., incl. Ted Hughes, *The Hawk in the Rain*], *New S*, LIV (Sept. 28), 391-92.

C1248 "Dialogue" [P.], *New S*, LIV (Nov. 2), 572.

C1249 "Rilke's Genius" [R., Rainer Maria Rilke, *Poems*, trans. J. B. Leishman], *Observer*, No. 8679 (Nov. 3), p. 15.

C1250 "The Novelist" [R., Henry James, *The House of Fiction*, ed. Leon Edel], *Observer*, No. 8682 (Nov. 24), p. 19.

C1251 "Stream and Lake" [R.], *New S*, LIV (Dec. 7), 785-86.

C1252 "Poet of Vision" [R., *The Divine Vision* (ed. Vivian de Sola Pinto; G. W. Digby, *Symbol and Image in William Blake*], *Observer*, No. 8686 (Dec. 22), p. 11.

C1253 "Books of the Year," *Observer*, No. 8686 (Dec. 22), p. 10.
Muir's choices were Lawrence Durrell, *Bitter Lemons*; Anthony Powell, *At Lady Molly's*; Ted Hughes, *The Hawk in the Rain*.

C1254 "Toys and Abstractions" [E.], *Saltire Rev*, IV (Winter), 36-37.

1958

C1255 "Pagan Paradise Lost" [R., Roy Campbell, *Collected Poems*, Vol. II), *New S*, LV (Jan. 11), 49-50.

C1256 "Ruthless Interpreter" [R., F. A. C. Wilson, *W. B. Yeats and Tradition*], *Observer*, No. 8689 (Jan. 12), p. 15.

C1257 "Nooks of Scotland" [E.], *Listener*, LIX (Jan. 16), 120.

C1258 "New Verse" [R.], *New S*, LV (Jan. 18), 76-77.

C1259 "Penelope in Doubt" [P.], *Listener*, LIX (Jan. 23), 152.

C1260 "Sick Caliban" [P.], *Listener*, LIX (Feb. 6), 244.

C1261 "Life in the South" [R., William Faulkner, *The Town* and *The Hamlet*], *Observer*, No. 8693 (Feb. 9), p. 15.

C1262 "Michael Roberts" [R., Michael Roberts, *Collected Poems*], *New S*, LV (Feb. 22), 246.

C1263 "Changing the Style" [R., *The Variorum Edition of the Poems of W. B. Yeats*, ed. Peter Allt and Russell K. Alspach], *Observer*, No. 8700 (March 30), p. 16.

C1264 "Critical Insight" [R., A. Alvarez, *The Shaping Spirit*], *Observer*, No. 8703 (April 20), p. 16.

C1265 "Bourgeois and Artist" [R.], *New S*, LV (April 26), 536.

C1266 "New Verse" [R.], *New S*, LV (May 3), 574.

C1267 "The Missing Epic" [R., E. M. W. Tillyard, *The Epic Strain in the English Novel*], *Observer*, No. 8706 (May 11), p. 17.

C1268 "Light on Dark" [R.], *Observer*, No. 8709 (June 1), p. 16.

C1269 "The Last War" [P.], *New S*, LV (June 4), 770.

C1270 "Landor Reassessed" [R., Malcolm Elwin, *Landor, A Replevin*], *Observer*, No. 8711 (June 15), p. 17.

C1271 "Facts and Flytings" [R.], *New S*, LV (June 18), 840.

C1272 "Poetic Imagery" [R., R. A. Foakes, *The Romantic Assertion*], *Observer*, No. 8716 (July 20), p. 15.

C1273 "Re-Reading Proust: The Famous Madeleine" [R., Marcel Proust, *Swann's Way*, trans. C. K. Scott Moncrieff], *Observer*, No. 8724 (Sept. 14), p. 17.

C1274 "Voice and Manner" [R.], *New S*, LVI (Sept. 20), 387-88.

C1275 "The Pretender" [R., Thomas Wolfe, *Selected Letters of Thomas Wolfe* (ed. Elizabeth Nowell) and *Look Homeward, Angel*], *Observer*, No. 8725 (Sept. 21), p. 18.

C1276 "Awake in Heaven" [R., *Thomas Traherne: Centuries, Poems and Thanksgivings*, ed. H. M. Margoliouth], *Observer*, No. 8727 (Oct. 5), p. 20.

C1277 "Dottor Serafico" [R., *The Letters of Rainer Maria Rilke and Princess Marie von Thurn und Taxis*, trans. Nora Wydenbruck], *New S*, LVI (Oct. 18), 536-37.

C1278 "Method and Art" [R.], *Observer*, No. 8730 (Oct. 26), p. 21.

C1279 "Endurance Point" [R., A. E. Ellis, *The Rack*], *Observer*, No. 8732 (Nov. 9), p. 21.

1959

C1280 "Last Poems: The Day before the Last Day. I have been taught," *Encounter*, XII (June), 3-4.

C1281 "The Poet" [P.], *New S*, LVIII (Oct. 3), 434.

1960

C1282 "Penelope in Doubt" [P.], *Encounter*, XIV (March), 61.

ADDENDA

ADDENDA

D. TRANSLATIONS
BY EDWIN AND WILLA MUIR

The following translations have been arranged according to the year of the first London publication, even though in some cases the American edition was actually earlier, and, in other cases, the American publisher contracted for the translation. The translations are from German, with the exceptions of D31, which is from the French, and D34 and D36, which are the Muirs' revisions of translations made by other writers from the Hungarian.

D. TRANSLATIONS
BY EDWIN AND WILLA MUIR

1925

D1   Gerhart Hauptmann, *The Dramatic Works*. Vol. VIII, *Poetic Dramas*. Martin Secker (June). 480 pp.
Contains *Indipohdi, The White Saviour*, and *A Winter Ballad*.
Published in America by B. W. Huebsch, 1925.

D2   Gerhart Hauptmann, *The Island of the Great Mother*. Martin Secker (December). 256 pp.
Published in America by the Viking Press, 1925.

1926

D3   Lion Feuchtwanger, *Jew Süss*. Martin Secker (November). 424 pp.
Published in America as *Power* by the Viking Press, 1926.

1927

D4   Lion Feuchtwanger, *The Ugly Duchess*. Martin Secker (November). 312 pp.
Published in America by the Viking Press, 1928.

1929

D5   Lion Feuchtwanger, *Two Anglo-Saxon Plays: The Oil Islands* and *Warren Hastings*. Martin Secker (April). 241 pp.
Published in America by the Viking Press, 1928.

D6   Gerhart Hauptmann, *The Dramatic Works*. Vol. IX, *Historic and Legendary Dramas*. Martin Secker (June). 386 pp.
Published in America by the Viking Press, 1929.

Contains *Veland*, translated by Edwin Muir; and *Florian Geyer*, translated by B. Q. Morgan. *Veland* is the only work which Muir translated by himself.

D7   Ludwig Renn [*i. e.*, Arnold Friedrich, Vieth von Golssenau], *War*. Martin Secker (June). 364 pp.
      Published in America by Dodd, 1929.

D8   Ernst Glaeser, *Class of 1902*. Martin Secker (October). 326 pp.
      Published in America by the Viking Press, 1929.

1930

D9   Franz Kafka, *The Castle*. Martin Secker (March). 451 pp.
      Published in America by Knopf, 1930.

D10   Emil Alphons Rheinhardt, *The Life of Eleonora Duse*. Martin Secker (March). 292 pp.

D11   Lion Feuchtwanger, *Success*. Martin Secker (November). 740 pp.
      Published in America by the Viking Press, 1930.

1931

D12   Ludwig Renn, *After War*. Martin Secker (January). 288 pp.
      Published in America by Dodd, 1931. *Cf.* D7.

1932

D13   Kurt Heuser, *Inner Journey*. Martin Secker (May). 320 pp.
      Published in America as *Journey Inward* by the Viking Press, 1932.

D14   Hermann Broch, *The Sleepwalkers*. Martin Secker (October). 648 pp.
      Published in America by Little, 1932.

D15   Lion Feuchtwanger, *Josephus*. Martin Secker (October). 504 pp.
      Published in America by the Viking Press, 1932.

1933

D16   Franz Kafka, *The Great Wall of China, and other pieces*. Martin Secker (May). 285 pp.

D17   Ernst Lothar, *Little Friend*. Martin Secker (June). 357 pp.
      Published in America by Putnam, 1933.

D18 Shalom Asch, *Three Cities*. Gollancz (October). 899 pp.
Published in America by Putnam, 1933.

1934

D19 Heinrich Mann, *Hill of Lies*. Jarrolds (April). 288 pp.
Published in America by Dutton, 1935.

D20 Shalom Asch, *Salvation*. Gollancz (September). 446 pp.
Published in America by Putnam, 1934.

1935

D21 Shalom Asch, *Mottke the Thief*. Gollancz (September). 314 pp.
Published in America by Putnam, 1935.

D22 Hermann Broch, *The Unknown Quantity*. Collins (September).
240 pp.
Published in America by the Viking Press, 1935.

D23 Ernst Lothar, *The Mills of God*. Martin Secker (September). 308
pp.
Published in America as *The Loom of Justice* by Putnam, 1935.

D24 Lion Feuchtwanger, *The Jew of Rome*. Hutchinson (November).
600 pp.
Published in America by the Viking Press, 1936.

1936

D25 Erik Maria von Kühnelt-Leddihn, *Night Over the East*. Sheed and
Ward (March). 440 pp.
Published in America by the Oxford University Press, 1936. The
author's name is given only in the second edition, September, 1937.

D26 Robert Neumann, *The Queen's Doctor*. Gollancz (May). 401 pp.
Published in America by Knopf, 1936.

D27 Shalom Asch, *Calf of Paper*. Gollancz (September). 590 pp.
Published in America as *War Goes On* by Putnam, 1936.

1937

D28 Lion Feuchtwanger, *False Nero*. Hutchinson (July). 478 pp.
Published in America as *Pretender* by the Viking Press, 1937.

D29   Franz Kafka, *The Trial*. Gollancz (July). 285 pp.
      Published in America by Knopf, 1937.

1938

D30   Robert Neumann, *A Woman Screamed*. Cassell (February). 375
      pp.
      Published in America by the Dial Press, 1938.
D31   Georges Maurice Paléologue, *Enigmatic Czar*. Hamilton (April).
      326 pp.
      Published in America by Harper, 1938.
D32   Franz Kafka, *America*. Routledge (October). 300 pp.
      Published in America by New Directions, 1940.

1940

D33   Carl Jakob Burckhardt, *Richelieu*. George Allen and Unwin (Feb-
      ruary). 413 pp.
      Published in America by Nelson, 1940.

      ["Translated by Willa and Edwin Muir" appears on the title page
      of Lion Feuchtwanger's *Paris Gazette*, New York, Viking Press,
      1940, but not in the English edition of the same work published
      by Hutchinson, March, 1940. Mrs. Muir has told me that she and
      her husband were not the translators.]

1941

D34   Zsolt Harsányi, *Through the Eyes of a Woman*. Routledge
      (March). 460 pp.
      Published in America as *Through a Woman's Eyes* by Putnam in
      1940. Although the Muirs are credited on the title page with being
      the translators, Mrs. Muir has told me that she cannot remember
      the novel and that very probably she and her husband rewrote the
      work of some less well-known translator. *Cf.* D36.
D35   Franz Kafka, "From Kafka's Diaries: Excerpts," *New S*, XXI
      (March 29), 321-22.
      This selection of excerpts was reprinted in the *SRL* (NY), XXIV
      (July 26), 3-4.

1942

D36 Zsolt Harsányi, *Lover of Life*. Translated from the Hungarian by Paul Tabor in collaboration with Willa and Edwin Muir. New York, Putnam. 678 pp.
Not published in England.

1947

D37 Franz Kafka, *Parables, in German and English*. New York, Schocken. 127 pp.
Part of this work was translated by Clement Greenberg.
Not published in England.

1948

D38 Franz Kafka, *In The Penal Settlement. Tales and Short Pieces*. Martin Secker. 298 pp.
Published in America by Schocken, 1948.

TRANSLATIONS BY WILLA MUIR: In addition to these translations which she made with her husband, Mrs. Muir was also responsible for a number of novels which were published as "Translated by Agnes Neill Scott." The British Museum Catalogue lists the following works under "Scott, Agnes Neill":

Hans Carossa: *A Roumanian Diary* (1929), *A Childhood* (1930), *Boyhood and Youth* (1931), *Doctor Gion* (1933);

C. Winsloe, Baroness Hatvany: *The Child Manuela* (1933), *Life Begins* (1935).

Mrs. Muir translated the following items under her own name:

Hermann Broch, "A Passing Cloud," *Modern Scot*, IV (Jan., 1934), 304-12.

Franz Kafka, "First Sorrow," *European Qtly*, I (May, 1934), 46-49.

"Selections from Diaries and Notebooks of Franz Kafka," *Orion*, I (Spring, 1945), 104-15.

ADDENDA

INDEX OF POEMS AND ESSAYS

INDEX OF POEMS AND ESSAYS

ADDENDA

ADDENDA

ADDENDA

ADDENDA

ADDENDA

SUPPLEMENT

to

Bibliography

of the

Writings of Edwin Muir

by

ELGIN W. MELLOWN

Incorporating Additional Entries

Compiled by PETER HOY

THE UNIVERSITY OF ALABAMA PRESS

University, Alabama 35486

KAYE & WARD LTD, LONDON

A Note
on the SUPPLEMENT to
Bibliography of the Writings of Edwin Muir

SINCE THE *Bibliography* was published in 1964, I have obtained further information that corrects or supplements the data presented therein; and, through the kindness of various correspondents, fellow-students and admirers of Edwin Muir, I have learned of writings by him that were omitted from the 1964 listing. While economic considerations make it impossible at this time to reissue the *Bibliography* in revised form, this Supplement brings the 1964 edition up to date and provides the most complete list of Muir's writings available.

I have arranged this Supplement in the form of the *Bibliography*, the numbers assigned indicating the place of the new entries in the chronology of Muir's career. The entries in Part A generally supplement or correct bibliographical details, although, having at last located a copy of the cheap edition of *John Knox* (A8), I have added a description of it, as well as descriptions of Muir's books published after 1964. Some of these entries were first published in the British edition of the *Bibliography* (London: Nicholas Vane Ltd., 1966).

The numerous additions in Sections B and C are mainly the work of Mr. Peter Hoy, Merton College, Oxford, who first published them in the *Serif* (VI [June, 1969], 27-32). His contributions are included with his permission and are identified by his name. Other entries were sent to me by Professor Peter Butter or were listed by him in the *Times Literary Supplement* (No. 3369, Sept. 22, 1966, p. 888) ; they are identified by his name. I am sure that both my collaborators would agree with me that these listings cannot be considered to include all of Muir's contributions to newspapers and journals and that other writings, particularly in newspapers, are yet to be identified.

While I regret not being able to include here a list of critical writings about Muir, I have published such a list in the *Bulletin of Bibliography* (XXV [1968], 157-60, 173-75), and it has been augmented by Peter Hoy in the *Serif* (VII [March, 1970], 11-19).

In my original Preface I suggested that Mrs. Muir possessed copies of her husband's lectures; regretfully I must report that she subsequently informed me that Muir's lectures at Bristol, Newbattle Abbey, Rome, and Prague were delivered "off the cuff, without a script."

ELGIN W. MELLOWN

Duke University
Summer, 1970

A. BOOKS AND PAMPHLETS

A1   WE MODERNS   1918

a. First English Edition

Correction: On the label of the later bindings there is a double rule at bottom and top (as opposed to the single rule on the earlier label) ; "AND " is replaced by an ampersand; and upper-case "BY" is replaced by lower-case "by."

A2   LATITUDES   1924

a. First English Edition

Addition: Blue dust-jacket printed in black with advertisements on back cover.

A3   FIRST POEMS   1925

a. First English Edition

Correction: Pagination should read: P. [1] half-title . . . *stet* . . . pp. 9-42, text; p. [43] section title: Ballads; p. [44] blank; pp. 45-74, [75] text; p. [75] * Printed in Great Britain by Neill and Co., Ltd., Edinburgh; p. [76] blank.

The ornament on the title-page is the device of Huebsch, publisher of the American edition (A3*b*) : the seven-branched candelabra with the initials B. W. H.

b. First American Edition

Correction: Identical with A3*a* with these exceptions: the outer leaves of signatures [1] and 5 are not pasted down, and there is thus one blank leaf before the half-title and one blank leaf after p. [76].

Addition: Grey dust-jacket printed in black; photograph of Muir on front cover.

A4   CHORUS OF THE NEWLY DEAD   1926

First Edition

Addition: Leonard Woolf in *Downhill All the Way* (London: Hogarth Press, 1968, pp. 130-32) gives important details concerning his relationship to Muir and the publication of this book, including the fact that 315 copies were printed and bound by himself and Mrs. Woolf, the price of each being 2s. 6d. In a year's time 215 copies were sold.

A6   THE MARIONETTE   1927

b. First American Edition.   1927

Correction: Published 1927. $1.75

A7   THE STRUCTURE OF THE NOVEL   1928

a. First English Edition

 Addition: P. 151; * Printed in Great Britain by Neill and Co., Ltd., Edinburgh.

Binding: Also bound in orange cloth boards lettered in red; front cover as noted for paper-binding with the publisher's wolf-head device in center between "EDWIN MUIR" and "THE HOGARTH PRESS," the whole enclosed by an ornamental rule; spine lettered in red: THE STRUCTURE | OF | THE NOVEL | EDWIN MUIR | THE HOGARTH | PRESS; end-papers.

b. First American Edition.   1929

Addition: Blind-stamped lettering on front cover enclosed within ornamental, blind-stamped border; lettering on spine as noted, with HARCOURT | BRACE & CO. at bottom.

a. First English Edition

b. First American Edition.   1929

Correction: Top and fore edges trimmed; bottom untrimmed.
Addition:

c. Second English Issue.   1930

THE LIFE AND LETTER SERIES NO. 12 | * | EDWIN MUIR |
JOHN KNOX: | PORTRAIT OF A CALVINIST | WITH FOUR
ILLUSTRATIONS | LONDON • JONATHAN CAPE • TORONTO

316 pp.   7¾ x 5¼ in.

P. [i] half-title; p. [ii] two-paragraph description of the Life and Letters
Series; frontispiece facing p. [iii]; p. [iii] title; p. [iv] First published
1929 | Re-issued in | The Life and Letters Series | 1930 | Printed in Great
Britain by | Lowe and Brydone (Printers) | Ltd. London, * * N. W. 1;
pp. [v]-316, identical with A8*a*; no blank leaves at end.

Green cloth boards lettered in silver; on front: * JOHN KNOX * with
ornament in lower left corner; on spine: JOHN | KNOX | * | EDWIN |
MUIR | JONATHAN CAPE; all edges trimmed; end-papers.

Published 1930.   4s. 6d.

CONTENTS: As for A8*a*.

Correction: No preliminary blank leaf; p. [4] All rights reserved | Printed
in Great Britain | by The Camelot Press Southampton | for | J. M. Dent
& Sons Ltd. | Aldine House Bedford St. London | Toronto • Vancouver |
Melbourne • Auckland | First Published 1932; each section title on an
unnumbered recto with blank verso; one blank leaf following p. 254.

Lettering on spine includes * between "TOM" and "EDWIN MUIR."
White dust-jacket printed in blue and black; abstract design on spine
and front cover; description of novel on inside front flap; publisher's
advertisement on back cover and inside back flap.

A13   SCOTTISH JOURNEY   1935

First Edition

Addition: CONTENTS: Scottish Journey [introduction]. Chapters I. Edinburgh (includes poem, "Now the frost lays its smooth claws on the sill"); II. The South; III. To Glasgow (includes poems, "Scottish cattle are sleek and proud" and "The women talk, tea-drinking by the fire"); V. The Highlands; VI. Conclusion.

A16   JOURNEYS AND PLACES   1937

First Edition

Correction: p. [iv] All rights reserved | Made in Great Britain | at The Temple Press Letchworth | for | J. M. Dent & Sons Ltd. | Aldine House Bedford St. London | First Published 1937; pp. 3-53, [54], text.

A17   THE PRESENT AGE   1939

a. First English Edition

Correction: P. [8] First published 1939 | Printed in Guernsey, C. I., British | Isles, by the Star and Gazette Ltd.

Spine lettered in blue: THE | PRESENT AGE | EDWIN MUIR | THE | CRESSET | PRESS

A18   THE STORY AND THE FABLE   1940

First Edition

Addition: White dust-jacket printed in blue and rose; publisher's blurb on inside front flap; advertisement on back cover.

A19   THE NARROW PLACE   1943

First Edition

Addition: Light-green dust-jacket printed in red; blurb on inside front flap; publisher's advertisement on back cover.

A22   THE POLITICS OF KING LEAR   1947

First Edition

Correction: P. 24: line divisions occur only between "Ltd." and "The," and between "Co." and "(Booksellers)."

A23   ESSAYS ON LITERATURE AND SOCIETY   1949

b. Second English Edition. 1965

ESSAYS ON | LITERATURE | AND | SOCIETY | BY | EDWIN MUIR | ENLARGED AND REVISED | EDITION | * | THE HOGARTH PRESS | LONDON

240 pp.   8½ x 5½ in.

Pp. [1-2] blank; p. [3] half-title; p. [4] By the same Author (eight titles) ; p. [5] title; p. [6] Published by | The Hogarth Press Ltd. | 42 William IV Street | London W.C.2 | * | Clarke, Irwin & Co. Ltd. | Toronto | First published 1949 | This Enlarged and Revised Edition | First published 1965 | Edwin Muir 1949 and | © The Hogarth Press Ltd. 1965 ; pp. [7-8] contents; p. [9] section title: I; pp. 10-83, text; p. [84] blank; p. [85] section title: II; pp. 86-164, text; p. 165, section title: III; pp. 166-235, text; p. [236] blank; pp. 237-[240] Index; p. [240] Printed in Great Britain | By R. & R. Clark, Ltd., Edinburgh.

Blue cloth boards; spine lettered in gold: ESSAYS | ON | LITERATURE | AND | SOCIETY | * | EDWIN | MUIR | THE | HOGARTH | PRESS; all edges trimmed; end-papers. Cream-coloured dust-jacket printed in black and blue and flecked with tiny red markings; publisher's advertisement on inside; on back cover biographical information and picture of Muir.

Published February, 1965.   30s.

The revisions in this completely reset text were made by Edwin Muir and consist mainly of deletions of sentences or paragraphs; all poetry quotations are printed in italic type. The six new essays may be considered to be in their final form since, according to Mrs. Muir, they "were all in typed manuscript" when her husband died.

CONTENTS: As for A23*a*, with a third section consisting of: Panurge and Falstaff. Emma Bovary and Becky Sharp. Jane Austen. The Dark Felicities of Charles Dickens. The Poetic Imagination. A View of Poetry. [revised] Index.

c. American Second Edition. 1965

ESSAYS ON | LITERATURE | AND | SOCIETY | BY | EDWIN MUIR | ENLARGED AND REVISED | EDITION | HARVARD UNIVERSITY PRESS | CAMBRIDGE, MASSACHUSSETTS | 1965

240 pp.   8½ x 5½ in.

(Identical with A23*b*, with these exceptions: p. [5] title; p. [6] First published 1949 | This Enlarged and Revised Edition | First published 1965 | © Edwin Muir 1949 and | The Hogarth Press Ltd. 1965 | Printed in Great Britain.

Blue cloth boards; spine lettered in gold: ESSAYS | ON | LITERA-TURE | AND | SOCIETY | * | EDWIN | MUIR | HARVARD; all edges trimmed; end-papers. Dust-jacket as for A23*b*, but with Harvard University Press advertisement on inside back cover.

Published 1965. $5.25

CONTENTS: As for A23*b*.

A27   AN AUTOBIOGRAPHY   1954

b. First American Edition.   1945

Addition: Dust-jacket similar to that for A27*a* with name of publisher changed.

c. Second English Issue.   1964 [*1965*]

AN | AUTOBIOGRAPHY | * | EDWIN MUIR | UNIVERSITY PAPERBACKS | * | METHUEN: LONDON

288 pp.   8⅛ x 5⅛ in.

P. [1] half-title, including publisher's blurb, quotations from the *Specta-tor* and the *Sunday Times*, and series title, University Paperbacks | UP 102; p. [2] By the Same Author (thirteen titles); p. [3] title; p. [4]

First published by The Hogarth Press 1940 | Revised edition 1954 |
First published in this series 1964 | Printed in Great Britain | For copy-
right reasons this book may only be issued | to the public on loan or other-
wise in its original, soft | cover. A hardbound, library edition is also avail-
able | from The Hogarth Press. | University Paperbacks are published by |
Methuen & Co Ltd | 11 New Fetter Lane London EC4; pp. [5]-[288]
identical with A27*a*; p. [288] Printed in Great Britain | by Lowe &
Brydone (Printers) Ltd., London; eight unnumbered leaves with list of
Methuen's University Paperbacks (82 titles).

White, glossy paper covers printed in red and black; design on front
cover includes photograph of Muir (a detail from the photograph on the
dust-jacket of A27*a* and *b*) and lettering: PRICE 15 S NET IN U. K.
ONLY | * UNIVERSITY PAPERBACKS | EDWIN | MUIR | AN AU-
TOBIOGRAPHY; spine lettered from head to tail: * EDWIN MUIR:
AN AUTOBIOGRAPHY UP 102; publisher's advertisement on back
cover; all edges trimmed; no end-papers. Leaves glued at spine.

Published April, 1965.   15s.

Although the date on the title page is 1964, the *English Catalogue of
Books*, XX (1966), gives April, 1965, as the date of publication.

CONTENTS: As for A27*a*.

A29   COLLECTED POEMS   1960

c. American Second Edition. 1965

EDWIN MUIR | * | COLLECTED POEMS | NEW YORK | OXFORD
UNIVERSITY PRESS | 1965

[iv], 310 pp.   8 x 5½ in.

(Identical with A29*b*, with these exceptions: p. [i] half-title; p. [ii] full-
page photograph with caption: Edwin Muir | A photograph taken in
1955 when he was 68; p. [iii] title; p. [iv] Copyright © 1960 by Willa
Muir | Preface Copyright © 1965 by E. V. Eliot | Printed in the United
States of America; p. [1] Dedication: To Willa; p. [2] blank; pp. [3-5]
Preface (four paragraphs) signed T. S. Eliot; p. [6] blank; pp. [7-16]
page numbers omitted but pages not otherwise changed; following p.
310 three blank leaves.)

Blue cloth boards; spine lettered in white: EDWIN | MUIR | * | COL-LECTED | POEMS | * | * | OXFORD; all edges trimmed; endpapers. White and olive patterned dust-jacket printed in blue; advertisement for this book on inside includes photograph of Muir.

Published 1965. $6.00

The Preface by T. S. Eliot was originally printed in the *Listener* [LXXI (May 28, 1964), 872] under the title "Edwin Muir: 1887-1959" and was accompanied by the poem "Horses" (C1184).

CONTENTS: As for A29*b*.

A31   SELECTED POEMS   1965

First Edition

SELECTED POEMS | EDWIN MUIR | WITH A PREFACE BY | T. S. ELIOT | FABER AND FABER | 24 RUSSELL SQUARE | LON-DON

96 pp.   7¼ x 4¾ in.

Pp. [1-2] blank; p. [3] half-title; p. [4] by the same author (four titles); p. [5] title; p. [6] First published in this edition mcmlxv | by Faber and Faber Limited | 24 Russell Square London W.C.1 | Printed in Great Britain by | R. MacLehose and Company Limited | The University Press Glasgow | All rights reserved | © this selection Faber and Faber, 1965 | For copyright reasons this book may not be issued on | loan or otherwise except in its original soft cover; pp. 7-8, contents; pp. 9-11, Preface (five paragraphs) signed T. S. Eliot; p. [12] blank; pp. 13-96, text.

Glued sheets in stiff, plastic-treated, white paper covers; design on front cover in black, red, and green includes in horizontal type: EDWIN | MUIR | SELECTED | POEMS | EDITED BY | T. S. ELIOT; and in vertical type: FABER PAPER COVERED EDITIONS; spine lettered in black, red, and green from head to tail: EDWIN MUIR * SELECTED POEMS * FABER; inside front cover, advertisement for this book; inside back cover, list of Faber paper covered editions; outside back cover, list continued; all edges trimmed.

Published July, 1965.   6s. 6d.

The Preface by T. S. Eliot is identical with that in A29c, with one additional paragraph explaining that the poems were selected as "representative of all aspects of [Muir's] work" and were taken from the *Collected Poems* (A29b).

CONTENTS: Betrayal. Autumn in Prague. October at Hellbrunn. Ballad of the Soul. Ballad of the Flood. The Hill. Hölderlin's Journey. Merlin. The Private Place. The Original Place. Then. The Refugees. Scotland 1941. The Narrow Place. The Good Man in Hell. The Grove. The Return of Odysseus. Robert the Bruce—*To Douglas in Dying*. The Annunciation. The Bird. The Escape. The Castle. Thought and Image. The Voyage. The Fathers. Reading in Wartime. Song of Patience. For Ann Scott-Moncrieff (1914-1943). The Labyrinth. The Journey Back. The Child Dying. The Good Town. The Absent. Song ('Sunset ends the day'). Milton. The Animals. The Days. Outside Eden. The Grave of Prometheus. Orpheus' Dream. The Killing. One Foot in Eden. Scotland's Winter. To Franz Kafka. The Difficult Land. Day and Night. The Horses. The Island. The Late Wasp. The Late Swallow. Song ('This that I give and take'). The Desolations. 'There's nothing here.' 'The heart could never speak.' 'The refugees born for a land unknown.' The Day before the Last Day. 'I have been taught.'

B. CONTRIBUTIONS TO BOOKS

(excluding selections reprinted in anthologies or other books)

1926

Ba1   "On the Impoverishment of Language" in *Atlanta's Garland. Being the Book of the Edinburgh University Women's Union, 1926.* Edinburgh. Pp. 128-138. (Butter, Hoy)

1936

B3a   "Walter Scott" in *The English Novelists. A Survey of the Novel by Twenty Contemporary Novelists.* Edited and introduced by Derek Verschoyle. London. Pp. 111-122.
Possibly a revision of C410. (Hoy)

1938

B3b   Fragments from a letter to Gwendolen Murphy [concerning "The Riders"] in *The Modern Poet.* An Anthology Chosen and Edited by Gwendolen Murphy. London. Pp. 168-170. (Hoy)

1942

B4a   "Edwin Muir" [biographical note] in *Twentieth Century Authors,* ed. Stanley J. Kunitz and Howard Haycraft. New York. Pp. 993-94.

1946

B5a   Letter to David Peat in *Autobiography of David* .... Edited by Ernest Raymond. London. P.16. (Hoy)

B5b   "Note [on John Holms]" in *Out of This Century. The Informal Memoirs of Peggy Guggenheim.* New York, Pp. 121-124. Early draft of a fragment of A18. (Hoy)

1947

B6a   "The Burns Myth" in *New Judgements: Robert Burns. Essays by Six Contemporary Writers.* Edited by William Montgomerie. Glasgow. Pp. 5-12. (Hoy)

1948

B7a   "Nové údobí anglické poesie" in Jirí Kárnet *and* Josef Nesvadba, *eds., Mezi dvema plameny. Nová anglická poesie.* Prague. Pp. 9-21. Introduction to a Czech anthology of contemporary British poetry, from Auden to Dylan Thomas. (Hoy)

B7b   "Preface" to *Festival of Britain 1951. Catalogue of an Exhibition of 20th-Century Scottish Books at the Mitchell Library, Glasgow.* Introduced by Robert O. Dougan. Glasglow. Pp. iii-iv. (Hoy)

B7c   "Introduction" to George Mackay Brown, *The Storm and Other Poems.* Kirkwall. P. 5. (Butter, Hoy)

1956

B7d   "Preface" to George Blake, *Annals of Scotland, 1859-1955.* Edinburgh (BBC). Cited by Duncan Glen, *Hugh MacDiarmid and the Scottish Renaissance* (1964), pp. 223-24.

1966

B10   [Personal letters and diary entries] Quoted by Peter Butter, *Edwin Muir*, Man and Poet (Edinburgh). Indexed under "Diary" and names of recipients.

C. CONTRIBUTIONS
TO PERIODICALS AND NEWSPAPERS

1922

C135a "Aphorisms," *Broom: An International Magazine of the Arts* (Rome), III (Sept.), 141-44. (Hoy)
Cf. C129.

1923

C145 "A Note on the Scottish Ballads."
Addition: Reprinted in *The Freeman Book*, ed. B. W. Huebsch. New York, 1924.

C163 "At the Sign of the Thistle: George Douglas" [E.], *Scottish Nation* (Montrose), I (July 3), 3, 8-9.
Letter of comment by Hector T. C. Munro (July 10), 15; Muir's reply (July 24), 12. *Cf.* A2, C150. (Hoy)

C165a "At the Sign of the Thistle: A Note on the Scottish Ballads" [E.], *Scottish Nation*, I (July 10), 3, 14-15.
Cf. A2, C145. (Hoy)

C168a "Ballad of the Flood" [P.], *Scottish Nation*, I (July 31), 5.
Cf. A3, A29, C162, A31. (Hoy)

C177a "The Assault on Humanism" [E.], *Scottish Nation*, I (Sept. 4), 6-7.
Article in reply by C. M. Grieve [Hugh MacDiarmid] (Oct. 16), 4-5; letter by F. V. Brandford (Nov. 13), 10. *Cf.* 160. (Hoy)

C180a "A Note on Friedrich Hölderlin" [E.], *Scottish Nation*, I (Sept. 11), 6-7, 15.
Cf. C170. (Hoy)

C196a "The Assault on Humanism Again" [E.], *Scottish Nation*, II (Nov. 6), 4. (Hoy)

C202a "The Lost Land" [P.], *Scottish Nation,* II (Dec. 4), 15.
Cf. A3, C258. (Hoy)

1924

C223a "The New Young" [E.], *Reviewer* (Richmond, Va.), IV (April), 163-68.

C223a "Edwin Muir and Francis George Scott: A Conversation", *Northern Review* (Edinburgh/London), I (May), 22-27.
Cf. C204. (Hoy)

C227a *"Sehnsucht* in German Poetry" [E.], *Northern Review,* I (June-July), 129-132.
Cf. C194. (Hoy)

C233a "The Conscientious Artist" [Obituary essay on Conrad], *Northern Review,* I (Sept.), 237-239. (Hoy)

1925

C293 "Czech Fiction" [R.], *Selected Czech Tales,* ed. Marie Busch and Otto Pick, *Nation,* XXXVII (Sept. 12), 708-09.

1931

C402a "Scottish Literature in 1931", *Scots Observer,* VI (Dec. 17).
Cited by Glen, *op. cit.,* p. 275.

1932

C404a "An Inaugural Letter to the Editor", *New English Weekly,* I (April 21), 23. (Hoy)

1933

C440 "Scottish Literature" [R., A. M. Mackenzie, *An Historical Survey of Scottish Literature to 1714*], *New S,* VI (Aug. 5), 164.

1934

C469 "The Prosperous Orkneys" [E.], *Spec,* No. 5518 (March 30), pp. 500-01. (Correction: Hoy)

C479a "Franz Kafka" [E.], *Life and Letters*, X (June), 341-51. (Hoy)

C481 Letters by W. S. Ferrie on July 12, Sept. 13, and Oct. 4; by Torrance on July 19; replies by Muir on July 12, July 19, and Sept. 27. (Additional information: Hoy)

C483a "Pastoral" [P.], *New English Weekly*, V (July 26), 349. (Hoy)

C496a "Book Reviews" [T. S. Eliot, *After Strange Gods*; Thomas Mann, *The Tales of Jacob;* Phyllis Paul, *The Children Triumphant; Aspects of Dialectical Materialism*; A. G. Street, *Land Everlasting & The Furrow*], *European Quarterly*, I (Nov.), 206-208.
These reviews are signed "E.M." Since Muir was, with Janko Lavrin, the editor of *The European Quarterly*, and since no other contributor had the same initials, it seems reasonable to assume that they were written by the poet. The second and fourth issues of the same periodical also have six unsigned reviews respectively, but it is not at all clear that they are the work of Muir. (Hoy)

C504a "The Direction of Poetry" [Review of *The Year's Poetry*, edited by Denys Kilham Roberts, Gerald Gould and John Lehmann], *The Author, Playwright and Composer* (London). XLV, No. 2 (Christmas), 52-53. (Hoy)

1935

C520a "Industrial Scene" [P.], *Time & Tide* (London), XVI (March 9), 344. (Hoy)

C531a "Slave Trade" [R., Arnold Lunn, *A Saint in the Slave Trade*: *Peter Claver*], *English Review*, LX (May), 617-618. (Hoy)

C586a "Social Credit and the Labour Party: A Letter to a Socialist" [E.], *New English Weekly*, VIII (Jan. 30), 306.
Extracts from A14. (Hoy)

C613 Correspondence also includes letter by Muir, (Nov.), 62. (Additional information: Hoy)

C616a "The Theme of Art" [R., *The Timeless Theme*, ed. Colin Still]", *Outlook* (Edinburgh), I (July), 78-81. (Hoy)

1937

C678a "Mr. Edwin Muir's Defence of Romantic Poetry," *Poetry Review* (London), XXVIII (May-June), 221-22.
An acocunt of Muir's address to the St. Andrews University Literary Society including four paragraphs of direct quotation. (Hoy)

C684a "Laurence Sterne" [E.], *Scot's Magazine* (Dundee), New Series, XXVII (July), 265-271.
Cf. A23. (Hoy)

C695a "Notes on the Way" [E.], *Time & Tide*, XVIII (Sept. 18), 1223-1225.
On Scottish culture, Scottish newspapers, Eric Linklater and Home Rule for Scotland. Letters of comment from M. Mc-Cracken (Sept. 25), 1258; Robert Hurd (Oct. 2), 1290; James Ewing (Oct. 2), 1290; and James S. Johnston (Oct. 23), 1401. (Hoy)

C696a "Notes on the Way" [E.], *Time & Tide,* XVIII (Sept. 25), 1255-1257.
On the processes of history. (Hoy)

C703 "Letters" ["I. Forgiveness now, about to be"] and ["II. Tried friendship must go down perforce"] [P.], *Lond Mer*, XXXVII (Nov.), 6-7.

1939

C795a "Views and Reviews: The Dreamer" [Essay on Walter de la Mare's *Behold This Dreamer*], *New English Weekly*, XV (June 22), 157-158. (Hoy)

C807 "The Refugees"
Correction: Only part of the last "Chorus" has been reprinted.

C807a "New Poetry" [R., Dylan Thomas, *The Map of Love*; Ronald Bottrall, *The Turning Path*; *New Verse*, edited by Geoffrey Grigson], *Purpose* (London), XI (Oct.-Dec.), 241-243. (Hoy)

1940

C823a "Criticising the Reviewer" [R., Frank Swinnerton, *The Reviewing and Criticism of Books*], *New English Weekly*, XVI (April 11), 369-370. (Hoy)

C831a "Recent Poetry" [R., Ezra Pound, *Cantos LII-LXXI*; W. H. Auden, *Another Time*; George Barker, *Lament and Triumph*], *Purpose*, XII (July-Dec.), 149-152. (Hoy)

C837a "Yesterday's Mirror: Afterthoughts to an Autobiography" [E.], *Scot's Magazine* (Glasgow), XXXIII (Sept.), 404-410. (Hoy, Butter)

C841a "The Novel and the Modern World" [E.], *Horizon* (London), II (Nov.), 246-253. (Hoy)

1941

C853a "From the War Diary of Edwin Muir", *Decision* (New York), I (April), 31-33. (Hoy)

C868a *"New Year Letter.* By W. H. Auden" [R.], *Horizon*, IV (August), 139-143. (Hoy)

C878a "Literature and the Arts in Scotland", *Scottish Educational Journal* (Edinburgh), XXIV (Nov. 7), 739.
Verbatim report of an address given at the 'Art for the People' exhibition in the National Gallery, Edinburgh, October 1941. (Hoy)

1942

C890a "Poetry During War" [R., Stephen Spender, *Ruins and Visions*; Alun Lewis, *Raider's Dawn and Other Poems*], *Britain Today* (London), No. 72 (April), 24. (Hoy)

C897a "The Political Poets" [Essay on Auden, Day Lewis and Spender], *Britain Today*, No. 75 (July), 15-18. (Hoy)

1943

C910a "A Birthday" [P.], *Poetry Scotland* (Glasgow), No. 1 (1943), 12-13. (Hoy)

C920a "T. S. Eliot and His Time: The Homeless Generation" [E.], *Britain Today*, No. 86 (June), 21-24. (Hoy)

C925a "A 'Mature' Book: The Quality of *The Serpent*" [Essay on Neil M. Gunn's novel], *Scot's Magazine*, XXXIX (Aug.), 382-384. (Hoy)

1944

C952a "The Rider Victory" [P.], *Horizon*, X (Dec.), 376.
Cf. A21, A25, A29. (Hoy)

1945

C954a   "The Natural Man and the Political Man" [E.], *Penguin New Writing* (London), No. 26 (1945), 133-144.
      Cf. C897. (Hoy)

C954b   "Song of Patience" [P.], *Poetry Scotland*, No. 2 (1945), 12.
      Cf. A21 A29, A31. (Hoy)

C954c   "Later Poetry of T. S. Eliot" [E.], *Britain Today*, No. 105 (Jan.), 36-37. (Hoy)

C962a   "The Return" [P.], *New English Review* (London), XI (May), 35-36.
      Cf. A21, A25, A29. (Hoy)

1946

C975a   "Comfort in Self-Despite" [P.], *Scottish Art and Letters* (Glasgow), No. 2 (Spring), 23.
      Cf. A21, A25, A29. (Hoy)

C975b   "Epitaph" [P.], *Scottish Art and Letters*, No. 2 (Spring), 58.
      Cf. A21, A25, A29. (Hoy)

C975c   "Song of Sorrow; The Window" [P.], *Poetry Scotland*, No. 3 (July), 47-48.
      Cf. A21, A25, A29 for "The Window". (Hoy)

1947

C975a   "Laurence Sterne" [E. in Czech], *Listy* (Prague), I, iv (1947), 539-543. (Hoy)
      Cf. A23, C394, C684a.

C980a   "A Note on Franz Kafka" [E.], *Scottish Periodical* (Edinburgh), I (Summer), 3-6. (Hoy)

1948

C989a   "The Swimmer's Death" [P.], *New Athenian Broadsheet* (Edinburgh), No. 3 (April), *unpaginated*.
      Cf. A19, A15, A29, C895. (Hoy)

C989b   "The Absent; Circle and Square; The Intercepter; Head and Heart" [P.], *Scottish Periodical*, I (Summer), 109-112.
      Cf. A24, A25, A29 and A31. (Hoy)

C993a   "The Castle" [P.], *New English Review Magazine* (London), I, n.s., no. 4 (Dec.), 237.
       Cf. A21, A25, A29, C974, A31. (Hoy)

C993b   "A Nightmare Poem" [R., W. H. Auden, *The Age of Anxiety*], *Britain Today*, No. 152 (Dec.), 47-48. (Hoy)

1949

C1003a   "From a Poem 'The Journey Back'," *Poetry-London*, No. 15 (May), pp. 2-4.
       Stanzas 3, 4, and 7 of "The Journey Back". *Cf.* A24, A25, A29, A31, C991.

1950

C1026a   "William Wordsworth On the Occasion of His Birthday" [E.], *Britain Today*, No. 168 (April), 11-15. (Hoy)

C1033   "The New Literature" [R., Jean Paul Sartre, *What is Literature?* transl. Bernard Frechtman], *Observer*, No. 8300 (July 2), p. 7.

C1046a   "Stevenson the Storyman" [E.], *New Alliance & Scots Review* (Edinburgh), XI (Dec.), 165-166.
       Originally broadcast on the Scottish Home Service of the B.B.C. (Hoy)

1951

C1047a   "Scottish Culture and Adult Education", *Scottish Educational Journal*, XXXIV (Jan. 12), 28-30.
       A verbatim report of an address given at the 66th Congress of the Educational Institute of Scotland, December 28, 1950. (Hoy)

C1062a   "Too Much; The Transfiguration; Love in Time's Despite; The Debtor" [P.], *New Alliance & Scots Review*, XII (Aug.), 67.
       Cf. A24, A25, A29, C989. (Hoy)

C1069   "Sonnet" ["There's nothing here to keep me from my own.—"], *Listener*, XLVI (Sept. 27), 515.

C1078   "Sonnet" ["I who so carefully keep in such repair"], *Listener*, XLVI (Dec. 6), 964.

1952

C1083a "Poetic Drama in an Age of Prose" [R., T. S. Eliot, *Poetry and Drama*], *Britain Today*, No. 190 (Feb.), 40-41. (Hoy)

C1089a "W. H. Auden—The Latest Phase" [R., *Nones*], *Britain Today*, No. 193 (May), 41-42 (Hoy)

C1107 "A Great Austrian" [R., *Selected Prose of Hugo von Hofmannsthal*, transl. Mary Hottinger and Tania and James Stern], *Observer*, No. 8420 (Oct. 19), p. 8.

1953

C1114a "Dylan Thomas" [R., *Collected Poems, 1934-1952*], *Britain Today*, No. 201 (Jan.), 41-42. (Hoy)

C1123a "Outside Eden" [P.], *Irish Writing* (Cork), No. 23 (June), 50-51.
    Cf. A28, A29, A31. (Hoy)

C1123b "The Young Princes" [P.], *Harper's Bazaar*, LXXXVII (June), 88.
    Cf. A28, A29, C1116.

1954

C1148a "The Art of Dylan Thomas" [E.], *Harper's Bazaar*, LXXXVIII (Feb.), 128.

C1155 "Sonnet" ["I who so carefully keep in such repair"]; "Two Songs" ["Leave, leave your well loved nest" and "This will not pass so soon"], [P.], *Hudson Rev*, VII (Spring), 49-50.

C1159a "Milton" [P.], *London Magazine*, I (June), 15.
    Cf. A28, A29, A31. (Hoy)

1955

C1176a "The Tower" [P.], *Adam. International Review* (London), No. 250, p. 6.
    Cf. A29, C1218. (Hoy)

C1176b "The Riddle of Heine," *Observer*, No. 8535 (Jan. 2), p. 9. (Hoy)

C1194a "The Song" ["I was haunted all that day by memories knocking"], *London Magazine*, II (Aug.), 13-15.
    Cf. A29, C1212a. (Hoy)

1956

C1204a "Edwin Muir writes . . ." [Autobiographical notes], *Poetry Book Society Bulletin* (London), No. 9 (March), 1. (Hoy)

C1212a "The Song" ["I was haunted all that day by memories knocking"], *Harper's Bazaar*, XC (Sept.), 270-71.
Cf. A29, C1194a.

1958

C1272a "Two Poems: I. The Voices, II. Impersonal Calamity," *London Magazine*, V (Aug.), 11-12.
Cf. A29. (Hoy)

1959

C1279a "Poetry" [Essay on Burns], *Scottish Field* (Edinburgh), CVI (Jan.), 30-31. (Hoy)

C1280a "Sick Caliban; The Strange Return" [P.], *Poetry Book Society Bulletin*, No. 23 (Oct.), 2.
Cf. A29, C1222, C1260. (Hoy)

1963

C1283 "Poetry and the Poet" [E.], *Poetry Review* (London), LIV (Winter), 32-40.
Extract from A30. (Hoy)

1964

C1284 "The Horses" [P.], *Listener*, LXXI (May 28), 872.
Cf. A28, A29, A31, C1184. (Hoy)

1966

C1285 "Some Letters of Edwin Muir," *Encounter*, XXVI (Jan.), 3-10. These letters were written to Sydney Schiff between June, 1924, and January, 1939. On page 8, first column, line 30 should read "great as himself. Anthony was destroyed by a." Muir's poem "Impersonal Calamity" (A29, C1272a) is reprinted on page 10.

D. TRANSLATIONS
BY WILLA AND EDWIN MUIR

1932

D14 Hermann Broch, *The Sleepwalkers.*
Addition: Sections of this novel were published in periodicals:
"Distintegration of Values. Two selections from a long novel, *The
Sleepwalkers*, which will shortly appear in English, translated by
Edwin and Christina [*sic*] Muir," *Criterion*, XI (July, 1932),
664-75 (Hoy); also in the *Mod Scot* (see C407).

1933

D16 Franz Kafka, *The Great Wall of China, and other pieces.*
Addition: Published in America as *The Great Wall of China
Stories and Reflections* by Schocken Books, 1946. Selections were
included in *Selected Short Stories of Franz Kafka*, Introduction by
Philip Rahv, Modern Library, 1952, as well as in D37. The aphor-
isms entitled "He" were published by the *New English Weekly*,
II (Feb., 1933), 445-56 (Hoy); also in the *Mod Scot* (see
C411). The story "The Great Wall of China", with an introduc-
tion by Clement Greenberg, was published in *Commentary*, II
(Oct., 1946), 368-76. (Hoy)

1938

D30 Robert Neumann, *A Woman Screamed.*
Addition: A revised edition of this novel, entitled *Failure of a
Hero*, was published by Hutchinson's Universal Book Club, Lon-
don, in October, 1948. 256 pp.

1940

D33   Carl Jakob Burkhardt, *Richelieu.*
Addition: A revised edition, edited and introduced by Charles H. Carter, was published by Vintage Books (Random House), New York, 1964. 355 pp.

1948

D38   Franz Kafka, *In the Penal Settlement. Tales and Short Pieces.*
Addition: Selections were included in *Selected Short Stories of Franz Kafka*, Introduction by Philip Rahv, Modern Library, 1952. The story "The Metamorphosis" was reprinted with the original German text in a separate edition entitled *The Metamorphosis Die Verwandlung* by Schocken Books, 1968. 127 pp.

TRANSLATIONS BY WILLA MUIR (under her own name)
Five Songs from the Auvergnat Done into Modern Scots. Warlingham, Surrey, Samson Press, 1931. 100 copies. [8] pp.
Cf. A10.